First World War
and Army of Occupation
War Diary
France, Belgium and Germany

41 DIVISION
Headquarters, Branches and Services
Commander Royal Engineers
1 March 1918 - 31 October 1919

WO95/2624/2

The Naval & Military Press Ltd
www.nmarchive.com
Published in association with The National Archives

Published by

The Naval & Military Press Ltd

Unit 10 Ridgewood Industrial Park,

Uckfield, East Sussex,

TN22 5QE England

Tel: +44 (0) 1825 749494

www.naval-military-press.com

www.nmarchive.com

This diary has been reprinted in facsimile from the original. Any imperfections are inevitably reproduced and the quality may fall short of modern type and cartographic standards.

© Crown Copyright
Images reproduced by permission of The National Archives, London, England, 2015.

Contents

Document type	Place/Title	Date From	Date To
Heading	WO95/2624/2		
Heading	Headquarters, Royal Engineers, 41st Division. March 1918		
War Diary	Camposampiero (Italy)	01/03/1918	03/03/1918
War Diary	France	08/03/1918	08/03/1918
War Diary	Leucheux (France)	10/03/1918	19/03/1918
War Diary	Arras	20/03/1918	31/03/1918
Heading	Narrative Of Operations Of The 41st Div. R.E. from March 21st, 1918, to April 1st, 1918.		
Miscellaneous	Narrative Of Operations Of The 41st Div. R.E. From March 21st, 1918 To April 1st, 1918.	02/04/1918	02/04/1918
Heading	Narrative Of 41st Divisional Engineers 21st March To 1st April 1918.		
Miscellaneous	Narrative Of 41st. Division R.E. In Third Army Fighting 21st March-1st April 1918.		
Miscellaneous	Narrative Of Operations Of The 41st Div. R.E. From March 21st, 1918 To April 1st, 1918.	02/04/1918	02/04/1918
Miscellaneous	Brigade. 41st Division. VIIIth Corps. 4.4.1918.	04/04/1918	04/04/1918
Miscellaneous Map	41st VIIIth 7.4.1918.	07/04/1918	07/04/1918
Heading	C.R.E. 41st Division April 1918		
War Diary	Gaudiempre	01/04/1918	04/04/1918
War Diary	Steenwoord	05/04/1918	09/04/1918
War Diary	Ypres	10/04/1918	25/04/1918
War Diary	Vlamertinghe	26/04/1918	26/04/1918
War Diary	Poperinghe	27/04/1918	29/04/1918
War Diary	Lovie Ch.	30/04/1918	30/04/1918
War Diary	Lovie Chateau	01/05/1918	04/06/1918
War Diary	Nieurlet	05/06/1918	07/06/1918
War Diary	Eperlecques	08/06/1918	26/06/1918
War Diary	Oudezeele	27/06/1918	30/06/1918
Operation(al) Order(s)	Order No. 1 By C.R.E. 41st Division.	28/06/1918	28/06/1918
Miscellaneous	O.C. 228th Field Coy. R.E.	29/06/1918	29/06/1918
Heading	War Diary Of H.Q.R.E. 41st Division July 1918 Vol 27		
War Diary	Oudezeele	01/07/1918	01/07/1918
War Diary	La Linge Sht. 27. Belgium 1/40000.	02/07/1918	03/07/1918
War Diary	L.20.c.8.3.	04/07/1918	07/07/1918
War Diary	K.24.C.1.1.	08/07/1918	10/07/1918
War Diary	K.24.C.1.1. Belgium St. 27. 1/40000	11/07/1918	31/07/1918
Operation(al) Order(s)	Operation Order No. 2. By C.R.E. 41st Division.	14/07/1918	14/07/1918
War Diary	K.24.C.1.1. Belgium Sht. 27. 1/40000	01/08/1918	29/08/1918
War Diary	Wizernes	30/08/1918	31/08/1918
Operation(al) Order(s)	Operation Order No. 4 By C.R.E. 41st Division.	27/08/1918	27/08/1918
Operation(al) Order(s)	Operation Order No. 5 By C.R.E. 41st Division.	15/08/1918	15/08/1918
Operation(al) Order(s)	Operation Order No. 4. By C.R.E. 41st Division.	11/08/1918	11/08/1918
Operation(al) Order(s)	Operation Order No. 3 C.R.E. 41st Division.	01/08/1918	01/08/1918
Heading	War Diary Of H.Q.R.E. 41st Division September 1918 Vol 29		
War Diary	Wizernes	01/09/1918	03/09/1918
War Diary	Douglas Camp L14.a.20 Belgium Sheet 27.	04/09/1918	23/09/1918

Type	Description	Start	End
War Diary	Douglas Camp L.14a 2.0 Belgium Sht. 27 1/40000	23/09/1918	27/09/1918
War Diary	Mersey Cross Belgium Sht 28.6. 23c.7.5 1/40000	28/09/1918	29/09/1918
War Diary	Lock 8. I.32.a.9.5	30/09/1918	30/09/1918
War Diary	Fort Garry Belgium Sheet. 28 1/40000	09/10/1918	11/10/1918
War Diary	J.13.d.9.9.	12/10/1918	16/10/1918
War Diary	Ashmore Farm Belgium Sht 28 1/40000 L.15.C.9.0	17/10/1918	20/10/1918
War Diary	Poeselhoek Belgium Sht 29 1/40000 G 22.C 3.6.	21/10/1918	21/10/1918
War Diary	Hooghe N 9.b.15.15	22/10/1918	22/10/1918
War Diary	Hooghe Belgium Sht 29 1/40000 N.9.b.15.15	23/10/1918	27/10/1918
War Diary	Hoogman Foey. N.10.C.2.7	28/10/1918	28/10/1918
War Diary	Hoogman Foey Belgium Sht. 29 1/40000 N.10.C.2.7.	30/10/1918	31/10/1918
Heading	War Diary Of Headquarters R.E. 41st Division November 1918. Vol 31		
War Diary	Hoogman Foey Belgium Sht. 29 1/40000 N.10.C.2.7.	01/11/1918	02/11/1918
War Diary	St. Louis. I.34.d.9.7.	03/11/1918	07/11/1918
War Diary	Vichte	08/11/1918	10/11/1918
War Diary	Caster	11/11/1918	11/11/1918
War Diary	Boschgat	12/11/1918	12/11/1918
War Diary	Nederbrakel	13/11/1918	18/11/1918
War Diary	Santbergen	19/11/1918	21/11/1918
War Diary	Grammont	22/11/1918	30/11/1918
Heading	War Diary Of Headquarters R.E. 41st Division For December 1918 Vol 32		
War Diary	Grammont	01/12/1918	12/12/1918
War Diary	Enghien	13/12/1918	13/12/1918
War Diary	Hal	14/12/1918	14/12/1918
War Diary	Braine L'Alleud	17/12/1918	17/12/1918
War Diary	Marbais	18/12/1918	18/12/1918
War Diary	Mazy	19/12/1918	19/12/1918
War Diary	Waret La Chaussee	20/12/1918	20/12/1918
War Diary	Vinalmont	21/12/1918	31/12/1918
Heading	War Diary Of Headquarters R.E. 41st Division January 1919 Vol 33		
War Diary	Vinalmont	01/01/1919	07/01/1919
War Diary	Cologne	08/01/1919	31/01/1919
Heading	War Diary Of Headquarters R.E. 41st. Division February 1919 Vol 34		
War Diary	Cologne	02/02/1919	31/03/1919
Heading	War Diary Of Headquarters R.E. London Division April 1919		
War Diary	Cologne	01/04/1919	30/06/1919
Operation(al) Order(s)	C.R.Es Order No. G.1.	01/06/1919	01/06/1919
Miscellaneous	Appendix "A" (issued With C.R.E. London Division Order No. G.1 Dated 31/5/19).	31/05/1919	31/05/1919
War Diary	Cologne	01/07/1919	29/08/1919
War Diary	Wahn	30/08/1919	12/10/1919
Map	Map Issued With London Divn Order No. 294 Dated 24-5-19		
War Diary	Wahn	13/10/1919	31/10/1919

WO95/2624(2)

Returned from Italy
with Div. 3/8.3.18.

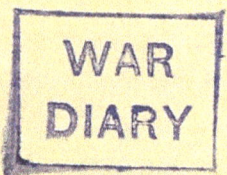
WAR DIARY

Headquarters,

ROYAL ENGINEERS, 41st Division.

M A R C H

1 9 1 8

Attached:-

Narrative of Operations,
21st March/1st April.

ORIGINAL

Army Form C. 2118.

WAR DIARY
or
INTELLIGENCE SUMMARY.
(Erase heading not required.)

HQrs RE 41st Division

No. 23

Instructions regarding War Diaries and Intelligence Summaries are contained in F. S. Regs., Part II. and the Staff Manual respectively. Title pages will be prepared in manuscript.

Place	Date	Hour	Summary of Events and Information	Remarks and references to Appendices
CAMPOSAM -PIERO (Italy)	March 1918 1st & 2nd		Divisional Headquarters at CAMPOSAMPIERO awaiting orders for entrainment to proceed to France	
	3rd		HQ RE entrained at CAMPOSAMPIERO with 233rd Field Coy RE	
FRANCE	8th		H.Q. R.E. detrained at MONDICOURT, near DOULLENS, and formed Divnl HQrs at LEUCHEUX	
LEUCHEUX (France)	10th		CRE visited HQrs IV Corps at GREVILLERS with AA & QMG	
"	11th		CRE visited Field Coys RE at PAS, OPPY and SOMBRIN	
"	12th		CRE visited III Army HQrs at ALBERT	
"	15th		Field Coys RE and Pioneer Battalion inspected by Divisional Commander	
"	16th		HQrs. RE carried out musketry practice on LEUCHEUX range	
"	17th		Orders issue received for Field Coys RE & Pioneer Battalion (5 Dorset) to work under 3rd CG III Army.	
"	18th		Proceed to ARRAS	
"	19th		CRE visited ARRAS defences and met Col Mallesom RE, CRE Rearzone III Corps	
"	19th		HQ RE work to ARRAS Adjutant (Capt Story RE) reported after short leave England	

Army Form C. 2118.

WAR DIARY
or
INTELLIGENCE SUMMARY.
(Erase heading not required.)

H Qrs RE 41st Division

March 1918

Place	Date	Hour	Summary of Events and Information	Remarks and references to Appendices
ARRAS	20		CRE visited work proposed on 4th line of defence in front of ARRAS with Major Nolan RE. Adjutant visits to 8 RE Park	
"	21		CRE visited work being done by Pioneers (19th Hussars) and by 228th Field Coy. RE	
"	22		CRE & Adjutant visited work of 237th & 233rd Field Coys RE on 4th line of Defences. Warning order received from C.E. III Army to cease work & prepare to move.	
"	23		HQrs RE moved to join Divl HQrs at BREWERS, field Coys moved to BERKELEY CAMP, near BIHUCOURT. Pioneer Battalion went into line under G.O.C. 123rd Inf Bde at midnight.	
	24th to 31st		Detailed account of all movements, work & fighting in which 41st Divisional Engineers took part on front of IV Corps is attached.	

J.M. Mooney
Lt Col RE
CRE 41st Divn.

5.4.18.

CRE 41st Divn.

NARRATIVE OF OPERATIONS of the 41st
Div. R.E. from March 21st, 1918, to
April 1st, 1918.

NARRATIVE OF OPERATIONS OF THE 41st DIV. R.E. from
MARCH 21st, 1918 to APRIL 1st, 1918.

1918.

March 19th. The Field Coys. R.E. and Pioneer Battalion (19th Bn. Middlesex Regt.) marched from LUCHEUX to ARRAS for work on 4th line of defences under C.E. Third Army.

March 20th. Work commenced on 4th line between CHANTECLEER and BEAURAINS and consisted in marking out trenches, digging posts and wiring.

March 21st & 22nd. Work on 4th line in front of ARRAS proceeded as above. A warning to cease work and prepare to move was received from C.E. Third Army.

March 23rd. Orders were received from 41st Division to proceed at once to BIHUCOURT and join the Division. Field Coys. R.E. and Pioneer Battalion left ARRAS 10.0.a.m. and reached BERKELEY and SAVOY CAMPS, BIHUCOURT at 8.30.p.m. C.R.E's Headquarters joined D.H.Q. at GREVILLERS. The Pioneer Battalion was ordered to join the 123rd Infantry Brigade who were in reserve in the neighbourhood of SAPIGNIES and thus were no longer available for work under the C.R.E. The 3 Field Coys. R.E. were ordered to construct a reserve line between SAPIGNIES and FAVREUIL. They commenced work at midnight in the following order -
237th Field Coy. R.E. under Major H.A.REID, M.C., R.E. on the right between H.22.a.0.4. and H.15.b.9.0.
233rd Field Coy. R.E. under Capt. M.D.R.HUNTER, M.C., R.E. in the centre between H.15.b.9.0. and H.9.d.7.4.
228th Field Coy. R.E. under Capt. E.P.ADAIR, M.C., R.E. bet on the left between H.9.d.7.4. and H.9.a.8.7.
The work ceased at daybreak, a considerable length of trench having been dug which was afterwards used to great advantage.

March 24th & 25th. Orders were issued for Field Coys. R.E. to work on IVth Corps RED LINE between FAVREUIL and BIEFVILLERS SPUR between BAPAUME-CAMBRAI Road and BIEFVILLERS-FAVREUIL Road. Field Coys. left BERKELEY CAMP, BIHUCOURT at 5.0.p.m. to commence work on this line; meanwhile Div.Hd.Qrs. had moved from GREVILLERS to ACHIET le PETIT; on arrival at the latter place fresh orders were received for the Field Coys. to construct a line of posts from N. corner of triangular wood N. of BIHUCOURT to the Cross Roads S. of GOMMECOURT. Cyclist orderlies were immediately sent out to recall the Field Coys. to BERKELEY CAMP while the C.R.E. and Adjutant reconnoitred this line of posts, returning to BERKELEY CAMP in time to meet the Field Coys. and take them to the new work. Shortly after midnight, while work was proceeding on this line of posts, orders were received by the C.R.E. for the Field Coys. to move immediately and take up a position on the right of 124th Infantry Brigade, who were withdrawing from BAPAUME, to the East of BIEFVILLERS and to get into touch with the 19th Division on their right thus filling the gap formed between the right of the 41st Division and the left of the 19th Division. The C.R.E. accordingly collected the Field Coys. and marched to BIEFVILLERS. At about 2.0.a.m. a position was taken up as follows; The 233rd Field Coy. R.E. from the BIEFVILLERS-BAPAUME Road just outside BIEFVILLERS village to the ACHIET le GRAND-BAPAUME Railway; The 237th FieldCoy. R.E. from the ACHIET le GRAND - BAPAUME Railway to the N.E. corner of GREVILLERS WOOD; The 228th Field Coy. R.E. in reserve in the sunken road on the Western side of BIEFVILLERS village. A continuous trench was dug to a depth of 3 feet along this line by daylight; S.A.A. and rations were then collected and distributed and the sappers continued to hold this until the attack had enveloped the village of BIEFVILLERS. At about 9.0.a.m. the enemy attacked heavily up the valley on the North of BIEFVILLERS from the direction of FAVREUIL and SAPIGNIES in force turning the flank of the village and causing the troops holding the RED LINE and Switch North and East of the village to retire through the village; at the same time the 19th Division on the right were seen to be retiring. It

It therefore became necessary for the Field Coys. to withdraw from their position and to take up with other troops a line from the Spur East of BIHUCOURT to the Railway Embankment and along it to the sunken road between BIEFVILLERS and GREVILLERS and back in a S.Westerly direction to GREVILLERS. This position was held for 1 hour and a half and considerable execution was done from it on the advancing enemy, eventually both flanks being in danger of being turned and the enemy having collected large numbers of machine guns in BIEFVILLERS and GREVILLERS it was necessary to withdraw to the next commanding ground which was being strongly held by a fresh battalion of the 25th Division on the Spur running through G.23.central. It was in this retirement, carried out under very heavy cross fire from machine guns, that the greater number of the casualties occurred. The R.E. passed through this battalion and reformed on the line of Tanks running from the railway bank at G.16.d. to G.27.central. This line was held by mixed troops until nearly dusk, when a retirement was made to the old German Line through G.15.central which was already held by the 5th Entrenching Battalion and other troops who had been collected and placed in this trench; this line covered the approaches to ACHIET le PETIT from the S.East. The remaining R.E. of the 41st Division then under the command of Major H.A.REID,M.C.,R.E. were then withdrawn to BUCQUOY, and thence to FONQUEVILLERS via GOMMECOURT, arriving there about 2.0.a.m. March 26th,1918.

March 26th. Div. Hd.Qrs. was now established at SOUASTRE; at about 10.0.a.m. a rumour was received to the effect that enemy cavalry had penetrated our lines in the neighbourhood of CAILLY AU BOIS and HEBUTERNE. All transport was therefore ordered to move in the direction of PAS. The R.S.M.,R.E. had been left at FONQUEVILLERS with orders to collect all stragglers of the 41st Division. These were added to the R.E. under Major REID and reinforced by such as had found their way to the transport lines at SOUASTRE. The Divisional Commander then ordered Major H.A.REID,M.C.,R.E. to take a position on the S.Side of FONQUEVILLERS through E.27.c.and d. facing the direction of SAILLY AU BOIS where they remained until receipt of orders through 123rd Infantry Brigade to withdraw to BIENVILLERS AU BOIS. C.R.E's Headquarters had meanwhile moved to BAILLEULVAL and Field Coys.transport under Capt. E.E.MARIETTE R.E. had bivouaced at LA CAUCHIE. Major H.A.REID,M.C.,R.E. established his Headquarters at BIENVILLERS AU BOIS at 1.0.a.m. March 27th.

March 27th. Field Coys. were placed under G.O.C. 123rd Infantry Brigade as Divisional reserve. The Division was holding a line in front of GOMMECOURT known as the PURPLE LINE. Div. Hd.Qrs. remained at BAILLEULVAL.

March 28th. Div. Hd. Qrs. moved to ST.AMAND. C.R.E's Headquarters and Field Coys. transport lines moved to GAUDIEMPRE. Sappers under Major H.A.REID,M.C.,R.E. remained at BIENVILLERS AU BOIS.

March 29th. Situation unchanged.

March 30th and 31st. 41st Division relieved the 42nd Division in the line at BUCQUOY. R.E. was placed in Divisional reserve under G.O.C. 122nd Infantry Brigade. Officers reconnaissances were made; R.E. dumps were formed at HANNESCAMPS and ESSARTS. At 3.0.p.m. Field Coys. R.E. moved to the RED LINE in F.20.b and d. Orders were given by G.O.C. 122nd Infantry Brigade for the R.E. to dig the portion of BROWN LINE from F.27.a. to F.26.central. Subsequently orders were received from Division that the R.E. duty was to clear out and wire the RED LINE in squares F.22.a., F.21.b., F.20.a.,b.,c., and d, and this work was continued on this line on March 31st.

1918.
April 1st.   Work was continued on the RED LINE as above; orders were received for relief of 41st Division by 42nd Division. R.E. on relief concentrated at transport lines at GAUDIEMPRE.

April 2nd.   Field Coys. R.E. joined Brigade Groups as follows:-

    228th Field Coy. R.E. to ORVILLE.
    233rd Field Coy. R.E. to THIEVRES.
    237th Field Coy. R.E. to FAMECHON.

Orders were received for entrainment on 3rd instant at PETIT HOUVIN station.

2nd April, 1918.   Lt. Colonel R.E.
                      C.R.E. 41st Division.

History 1/2   E/ in C. Files

Narrative of 41st Divisional Engineers
21st March to 1st April 1918.

Narrative of

41st Division R.E.

in Third Army fighting

21st March - 1st April 1918.

NARRATIVE OF OPERATIONS OF THE 41st DIV. R.E. from
MARCH 21st, 1918 to APRIL 1st, 1918.

1918.

March 19th. The Field Coys, R.E. and Pioneer Battalion (19th Bn, Middlesex Regt.) marched from LUCHEUX to ARRAS for work on 4th line of defences under C.E. Third Army.

March 20th. Work commenced on 4th line between CHANTECLERE and BEAURAINS and consisted in marking out trenches, digging posts and wiring.

March 21st & 22nd. Work on 4th line in front of ARRAS proceeded as above. A warning to cease work and prepare to move was received from C.E. Third Army.

March 23rd. Orders were received from 41st Division to proceed at once to BIHUCOURT and join the Division. Field Coys. R.E. and Pioneer Battalion left ARRAS 10.0.a.m. and reached BERKELEY and SAVOY CAMPS, BIHUCOURT at 8.30.p.m. C.R.E's Headquarters joined D.H.Q. at GREVILLERS. The Pioneer Battalion was ordered to join the 123rd Infantry Brigade who were in reserve in the neighbourhood of SAPIGNIES and thus were no longer available for work under the C.R.E. The 3 Field Coys. R.E. were ordered to construct a reserve line between SAPIGNIES and FAVREUIL. They commenced work at midnight in the following order -
237th Field Coy. R.E. under Major H.A.HAID, M.C., R.E. on the right between H.22.a.9.4. and H.15.b.9.0.
233rd Field Coy. R.E. under Capt. J.R.HUNTER, M.C., R.E. in the centre between H.15.b.9.0. and H.9.d.7.4.
228th Field Coy. R.E. under Capt. E.P.ADAIR, M.C., R.E. bet on the left between H.9.d.7.4. and H.9.a.8.7.
The work ceased at daybreak, a considerable length of trench having been dug which was afterwards used to great advantage.

March 24th & 25th. Orders were issued for Field Coys. R.E. to work on IVth Corps RED LINE between FAVREUIL and BIEFVILLERS SPUR between BAPAUME-CAMBRAI Road and BIEFVILLERS-FAVREUIL Road. Field Coys. left BERKELEY CAMP, BIHUCOURT at 5.0.p.m. to commence work on this line; meanwhile Div.Hd.Qrs. had moved from GREVILLERS to ACHIET le PETIT; on arrival at the latter place fresh orders were received for the Field Coys. to construct a line of posts from N. corner of triangular wood N. of BIHUCOURT to the Cross Roads S. of GOMMECOURT. Cyclist orderlies were immediately sent out to recall the Field Coys. to BERKELEY CAMP while the C.R.E. and Adjutant reconnoitred this line of posts, returning to BERKELEY CAMP in time to meet the Field Coys. and take them to the new work. Shortly after midnight, while work was proceeding on this line of posts, orders were received by the C.R.E. for the Field Coys. to move immediately and take up a position on the right of 124th Infantry Brigade, who were withdrawing from BAPAUME, to the East of BIEFVILLERS and to get into touch with the 19th Division on their right thus filling the gap formed between the right of the 41st Division and the left of the 19th Division. The C.R.E. accordingly collected the Field Coys. and marched to BIEFVILLERS. At about 2...a.m. a position was taken up as follows; The 233rd Field Coy. R.E. from the BIEFVILLERS-BAPAUME Road just outside BIEFVILLERS village to the ACHIET le GRAND-BAPAUME Railway; The 237th Field Coy.R.E. from the ACHIET le GRAND - BAPAUME Railway to the N.E. corner of GREVILLERS WOOD; The 228th Field Coy.R.E. in reserve in the sunken road on the Western side of BIEFVILLERS village. A continuous trench was dug to a depth of 3 feet along this line by daylight; S.A.A. and rations were then collected and distributed and the sappers continued to hold this until the attack had enveloped the village of BIEFVILLERS. At about 9.0.a.m. the enemy attacked heavily up the valley on the North of BIEFVILLERS from the direction of FAVREUIL and SAPIGNIES in force turning the flank of the village and causing the troops holding the RED LINE and switch North and East of the village to retire through the village; at the same time the 19th Division on the right were seen to be retiring. It

-2-

- 2 -

It therefore became necessary for the Field Coys. to withdraw from their position and to take up with other troops a line from the Spur East of BIHUCOURT to the Railway Embankment and along it to the sunken road between BIEFVILLERS and GREVILLERS and back in a S.Westerly direction to GREVILLERS. This position was held for 1 hour and a half and considerable execution was done from it on the advancing enemy, eventually both flanks being in danger of being turned and the enemy having collected large numbers of machine guns in BIEFVILLERS and GREVILLERS it was necessary to withdraw to the next commanding ground which was being strongly held by a fresh battalion of the 25th Division on the Spur running through G.23.central. It was in this retirement, carried out under very heavy cross fire from machine guns, that the greater number of the casualties occurred. The R.E. passed through this battalion and reformed on the line of Tanks running from the railway bank at G.16.d. to G.27.central. This line was held by mixed troops until nearly dusk, when a retirement was made to the old German Line through G.15.central which was already held by the 5th Entrenching Battalion and other troops who had been collected and placed in this trench; this line covered the approaches to ACHIET le PETIT from the S.East. The remaining R.E. of the 41st Division then under the command of Major H.A.REID,M.C.,R.E. were then withdrawn to BUCQUOY, and thence to FONQUEVILLERS via GOMMECOURT, arriving there about 2.0.a.m. March 26th,1918.

March 26th. Div. Hd.Qrs. was now established at SOUASTRE; at about 10.0.a.m. a rumour was received to the effect that enemy cavalry had penetrated our lines in the neighbourhood of SAILLY AU BOIS and HEBUTERNE. All transport was therefore ordered to move in the direction of PAS. The R.S.M.,R.E. had been left at FONQUEVILLERS with orders to collect all stragglers of the 41st Division. These were added to the R.E. under Major REID and reinforced by such as had found their way to the transport lines at SOUASTRE. The Divisional Commander then ordered Major H.A.REID,M.C.,R.E. to take a position on the S.Side of FONQUEVILLERS through E.27.c.and d. facing the direction of SAILLY AU BOIS where they remained until receipt of orders through 123rd Infantry Brigade to withdraw to BIENVILLERS AU BOIS. C.R.E's Headquarters had meanwhile moved to BAILLEULVAL and Field Coys.transport under Capt. E.S.MALDETTE R.E. had bivouaced at LA CAUCHIE. Major H.A.REID,M.C.,R.E. established his Headquarters at BIENVILLERS AU BOIS at 1.0.a.m. March 27th.

March 27th. Field Coys. were placed under G.O.C. 123rd Infantry Brigade as Divisional reserve. The Division was holding a line in front of GOMMECOURT known as the PURPLE LINE. Div. Hd.Qrs. remained at BAILLEULVAL.

March 28th. Div. Hd. Qrs. moved to ST.AMAND, C.R.E's Headquarters and Field Coys. transport lines moved to GAUDIEMPRE. Sappers under Major H.A.REID,M.C.,R.E. remained at BIENVILLERS AU BOIS.

March 29th. Situation unchanged.

March 30th and 31st. 41st Division relieved the 42nd Division in the line at BUCQUOY. R.E. was placed in Divisional reserve under G.O.C. 122nd Infantry Brigade. Officers reconnaissances were made; R.E. dumps were formed at HANNESCAMPS and SOUANTE. At 3.0.p.m. Field Coys. R.E. moved to the RED LINE in F.20.b and d. Orders were given by G.O.C. 122nd Infantry Brigade for the R.E. to dig the portion of BROWN LINE from F.27.a. to F.26.central. Subsequently orders were received from Division that the R.E. duty was to clear out and wire the RED LINE in squares F.22.a., F.21.b., F.20.a.,b.,c., and d, and this work was continued on this line on March 31st.

-3-

1918.
April 1st.   Work was continued on the RED LINE as above; orders were received for relief of 41st Division by 42nd Division. R.E. on relief concentrated at transport lines at DAUDIEMPRE.

April 2nd.   Field Coys. R.E. joined Brigade Groups as follows:-

   228th Field Coy. R.E. to ORVILLE.
   233rd Field Coy. R.E. to THIEVRES.
   237th Field Coy. R.E. to FAMECHON.

Orders were received for entrainment on 3rd instant at PETIT HOUVIN station.

M Hockley

2nd April, 1918.   Lt. Colonel R.E.
                                C.R.E. 41st Division.

Army Form W. 3121.

Schedule No. (to be left blank)	Unit	Regtl. No.	Rank and Name	Brigade. 41st	Division. VIIIth	Corps.	Date of Recommendation. 4.4.1918.		
					Action for which commended	Recommended by	Honour or Reward	(To be left blank)
	237th Field Coy. R.E.	—	Major Horace Arthur REID, M.C., R.E.		For most conspicuous gallantry on the 25th March, 1918, near GREVILLERS, when in command of his Company on the right flank of the Divisional front he disposed his men and others collected with them to the best advantage, and held his position until his ammunition was practically exhausted, and he was being hard pressed at close range; the enemy having mounted a machine gun in a tree overlooking his position. When retirement was ordered Major REID noticed a Captain of the 4th South Staffordshire Regt. who was wounded in the thigh lying in a shell hole in front of the line. Major REID went forward and took from him his revolver with which he was about to end his life, and assisted by Corpl. LONGHURST,R.E. carried this officer back to the line under heavy rifle and machine gun fire and retiring with his men finally handed him over to the charge of an American Medical officer attached to the Worcestershire Regt: a distance of about a mile. He then collected about 50 of his Company and having obtained fresh ammunition reformed them with several men of other units on a line taken up in a subsequent stage of the retirement, and did not withdraw until about 9.0.p.m. when orders for relief were issued. Major REID has throughout these operations shown marked courage, resource and military capacity, notably on the 24th March,1918, when ordered at 5.0.p.m. to proceed in command of the R.E. of the 3 Field Coys for work on the RED LINE from FAVREUIL to BIEFVILLERS Spur, he made a personal reconnaissance, and finding FAVREUIL 2.	Lt.Col.R.E C.R.E. 41st Divn.		

Army Form W. 3121.

Date of Recommendation.

Schedule No.	Unit	Regtl. No.	Rank and Name	Action for which commended	Recommended by	Honour or Reward	(To be left blank)
	237th Field Coy. R.E.	—	Major Horace Arthur REID, M.C.,R.E. (contd)	2. already evacuated put the party to work further down the line; and seeing the need for a defensive flank to the East laid out with the 23rd Bn. Middlesex Regt, and the 19th Bn. Middlesex Regt. (Pioneers) a switch line from the RED LINE to the BIEFVILLERS-BAPAUME Road which proved of great value.			

41st Brigade. VIIIth Division. Corps. 4.4.1918.

41st   VIIIth   7.4.1918.

237th Field Coy. R.E. — Lieut. Harry Elwood THOMAS, R.E. — For conspicuous gallantry and devotion to duty. On the night of 24/25th March,1918, near BIRDCOURT and BIEFVILLERS he showed a quick grasp of the situation. His example under fire was such as to inspire all those under him. The withdrawal of his men from the BIEFVILLERS-GREVILLERS Line was very well carried out. On reaching the ACHIET-le-PETIT Line he still had his men with him and was able to collect some stragglers, all of whom he kept in the line until relieved. He laid out and supervised the construction of the SIXTY LINE behind BUCQUOY and the wiring of the RED LINE in the same vicinity. During the night of 1st April 1918, he was instrumental in laying out 2,000 yards of wire in front of the RED LINE. Under the heaviest machine gun fire he showed great coolness and set a fine example to all ranks. Lt.Col.R.E. C.R.E. 41st Div. Military Cross.

(Recommended for immediate award.)

228th Field Coy. R.E. — 2/Lieut. Arthur BARKER, R.E. — For conspicuous gallantry on 25th March, 1918, near BIEFVILLERS when the Officer Commanding his Company was wounded and the next senior killed, he rallied his men and others adjacent to him and maintained a steady line with good fire effect until a general retirement was necessary. He then withdrew in good order and collected his men on the subsequent positions held until nightfall when relieved. Lt.Col.R.E. C.R.E. 41 Divn. Military Cross.

(Recommended for immediate award)

233rd Field Coy. R.E.	41st	VIIIth	7-4-1918.	

2/Lieut. Franklin WRIGHT. R.E.

For conspicuous gallantry and devotion to duty throughout the operations between 20th March and 1st April 1918, particularly on the 25th March when his Field Coy. was engaged in a rearguard action behind BIEFVILLERS. Owing to casualties he was left in sole charge of the Sappers of his Company and showed great coolness and enterprise in leading his Company through a very difficult situation requiring the utmost energy and courage.

Military Cross.

Lt.Col.R.E. C.R.E. 41st Div.

(Recommended for immediate award).

VIIIth   7.4.1918.

41st

228th Field   546099. Sapper Arnold
Coy. R.E.   William PICK.

For exceptional courage and endurance displayed
in bringing Capt. E.F.ADAIR,M.C.,R.E. back to
safety on the 25th March, 1918, while the Company
were resisting the German advance near AIRVILLERS.
During the retirement Sapper PICK remained
behind to carry Capt. ADAIR who had been wounded Lt.Col.R.E
the Germans were only about 100 yards away, but C.R.E. D.C.M.
Sapper PICK succeeded in carrying Capt. ADAIR 41st Div.
alone a few hundred yards on his back through a
storm of bullets. Capt. ADAIR was then wounded
a second time and he ordered PICK to put him
in a shell hole and make off. Sapper PICK would
not leave him, however, and assisted by 2/Corpl.
J.H.HOLLROYD who now appeared, succeeded in
bringing Capt. ADAIR to a R.A.P. more than a
mile back.

(Recommended for immediate award)

237th Field   137822. L.cpl. Herbert
Coy. R.E.   Ewart LONGHURST.

For conspicuous gallantry and devotion to duty
on 25th March,1918, near BIEFVILLERS. He was
instrumental in the saving of a badly wounded
officer in the face of a heavy cross machine gun
fire and a rapidly advancing enemy. The officer Lt.Col.R.E
was carried a distance of over 1 mile. all the   C.R.E.   D.C.M.
time under fire. Later, this N.C.O. rendered   41st Div.
great assistance in rallying troops and stragglers
in the ACHIET-LE-PETIT Line, and again worked
very hard on a trench system to the West of
BUCQUOY.

(Recommended for immediate award)

41st   VIIIth   7.4.1918.

233rd Field 131106. Sapper Herbert James For exceptional courage and devotion to duty
Coy. R.E.   WATERS.   throughout the operations of 41st Divn. between
                                                20th March,1918 and 1st April,1918. In particular
                                                at BIEFVILLERS on 23rd March,1918, in a rearguard
                                                action this sapper displayed the greatest bravery
                                                and was always one of the last to leave his posi-
                                                tion when a retirement to a fresh position was
                                                ordered. Finally, when the line was ordered to
                                                retire again,he went about 50 yards in front of
                                                this position under a withering machine gun fire
                                                with the enemy only 200 yards away and picked up
                                                a wounded man, and alone carried him back to the
                                                next line being held. Sapper WATERS then bound
                                                up the man's wounds, and with the aid of another
                                                man carried him back 3 miles on a stretcher to
                                                a dressing station.

                                                Lt.Col.R.E.
                                                C.R.E. 41st Div. D.C.M.

                                                (Recommended for Immediate award)

233rd Field 108618. Sergt. Richard   For untiring energy and courage throughout
Coy. R.E.   FLETCHER, M.M.   operations between 20th March and 1st April, 1918.
                                                On 25th March,1918, his coolness and bravery was
                                                particularly conspicuous, when his Company was
                                                fighting a rearguard action in rear of BIEFVILLERS.
                                                By his coolness and energy he rendered invaluable
                                                assistance in rallying his own men and others
                                                adjacent to him, inspiring them with confidence,
                                                and thereby helping to keep order in the retirement.

                                                Lt.Col.R.E.
                                                C.R.E. 41st Div. D.C.M.

                                                (Previous award:- Military Medal 29.6.1917)

                                                (Recommended for Immediate award)

41st   VIIIth   7.4.1918.

237th Field Coy. R.E.   137869. Sergt. Joseph COOPER.

For coolness and devotion to duty. At a critical moment on the morning of the 25th March when his section formed part of the troops of a line between BIEFVILLERS and GREVILLERS, and was ordered to retire to a position in the rear, this N.C.O. Lt.Col.R.E. steadied the troops in his vicinity, and due to C.R.E. D.C.M. his fine example of courage under fire, which was 41st Div. causing bad casualties, the retirement was effected in an orderly manner. Whilst thus doing his duty this N.C.O. was badly wounded.

(Recommended for immediate award)

7.4.1918.

41st VIIIth

237th Field 137929. L.cpl. Duncan   For conspicuous gallantry and devotion to duty
Coy. R.E.   Alexander CARPENTER,   on 25th March,1918, near SIEUVILLERS. This N.C.O
            M.M.   was one of a party that had been ordered to retire
                                      by Sergt. COOPER, but on seeing his sergeant
                                      badly wounded he at once turned and came to his   Lt.Col.R.E
                                      aid. He bandaged the sergeant in face of the
                                      enemy in the open under heavy machine gun fire,   C.R.E. Bar to
                                      and safely brought him in to a prepared line in   41st Div. M.M.
                                      the rear. The courage shown by this N.C.O. was
                                      most conspicuous.
                                      (Previous award:- Military Medal 12.10.1917.)

                                      (Recommended for immediate award).

228th Field 104514. Sapper Thomas   For his gallantry in bringing in Pioneer CAIRNS
Coy. R.E.   JORDON, M.M.   who was lying out in the open wounded during the
                                      German attack near BIEFVILLERS on 25th March, 1918.
                                      Sapper JORDON went out fully 100 yards and   Lt.Col.R.E
                                      succeeded in bringing Pion. CAIRNS into safety
                                      over ground offering no cover and under heavy   C.R.E. Bar to
                                      machine gun and rifle fire.   41st Div. M.M.
                                      (Previous award:- Military Medal 17.7.1917.)

                                      (Recommended for immediate award)

41st VIIIth 7.4.1918.

228th Field 120730. Corpl. Andrew   For gallant conduct in bringing in Sapper HARRIS   Lt.Col.R.E.
Coy. R.E.   Turnbull BROMFIELD. when the latter was wounded during retirement   C.R.E. Military
                                 on 25th March,1918. As the Company retired followed   41st Div. Medal.
                                 by the enemy, Sapper HARRIS was severely
                                 wounded. Corpl. BROMFIELD remained behind and
                                 carried him back to the dressing station.
                                 For fully 300 yards he was exposed to heavy
                                 machine gun fire. During the attack Corpl.
                                 BROMFIELD showed great coolness and kept his
                                 men well together.

                                 (Recommended for immediate award)

233rd Field 495508. Sapper James For conspicuous coolness and devotion to duty   Lt.Col.R.E.
Coy. R.E.   CAMBELL.   throughout the operations between 20th March   C.R.E. Military
                                  and 1st April,1918. In particular when the   41st Div.Medal.
                                  Company was billetted on the night of 21st
                                  March,1918, in ARRAS, during heavy shelling,when
                                  an estaminet was wrecked in the vicinity of the
                                  billets; this sapper rendered invaluable assis-
                                  tance and worked, tunnelling a passage, unceasingly
                                  for 3½ hours from the next house and rescuing men
                                  buried in the debris. During the whole of this
                                  period the neighbourhood was being heavily shelled.

                                  (Recommended for immediate award)

41st   VIIIth   7.4.1918.

228th Field Coy. R.E.	104363. 2/Corpl. John Edward HOLDROYD.	This N.C.O. volunteered to go back to find Capt. E.P.ADAIR,M.C.,R.E. who was wounded on 25th March,1918. After the Company retired on 25th March,1918. After looking in vain for a time he saw Sapper PICK bending down over someone. This proved to be Capt. ADAIR, whom Sapper PICK had carried back several hundred yards alone. Corpl. HOLDROYD then assisted Sapper PICK and together they carried Capt. ADAIR over a mile to a R.A.P. (Recommended for immediate award).	Lt.Col.R.E C.R.E. Military 41st Div. Medal.
233rd Field Coy. R.E.	108265. L.cpl. Frederick William COGGER.	For conspicuous devotion to duty throughout operations between 20th March and 1st April,1918. In particular when the Company were acting as Infantry holding a line for 8 days, this N.C.O. rendered invaluable service in organising and conducting ration parties and himself carrying food to the men in the line, often under heavy shell fire. (Recommended for immediate award)	Lt.Col.R.E C.R.E. Military 41st Div. Medal.

41st   VIIIth   7.4.1918.

237th Field 44523. Sapper John Arthur   For coolness and devotion to duty during opera-   Lt.Col.R.E.
Coy.R.E.   PARLEY.   tions from 22nd March to 1st April,1918. He was   C.R.E. Military
                                        an example to many by his coolness under fire,   41st Div. Medal.
                                        and the extraordinary amount of work he did, all
                                        of which was most useful. Though not a N.C.O.
                                        men in his vicinity always relied on his work
                                        and judgment, and he was thus of very great
                                        assistance to the officers and N.C.O's. His
                                        cheerfulness was most uplifting.

                                        (Recommended for immediate award)

237th Field 556033. Sapper William   For conspicuous gallantry and devotion to duty.   Lt.Col.R.E
Coy. R.E.   HOLLEY.   His cheerfulness and strength were most useful,   C.R.E. Military
                                        and he set a fine example under fire by his   41st Div.Medal.
                                        coolness on the 25th March,1918 near BIENVILLERS,
                                        when withdrawing to ACHIET-le-PETIT he assisted
                                        in bringing in a wounded comrade. His work during
                                        the period under review has been, as always,
                                        excellent.

                                        (Recommended for immediate award)

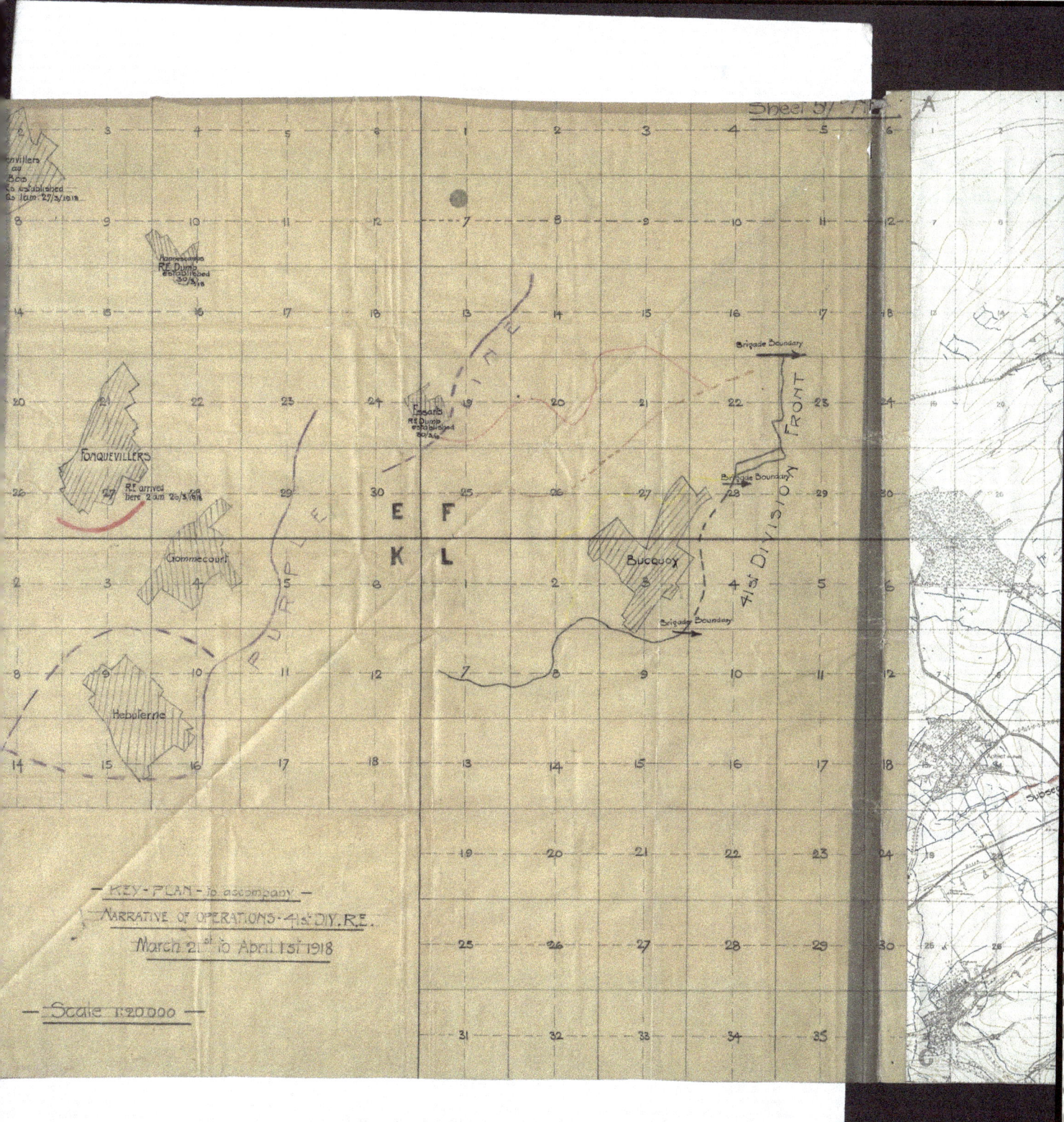

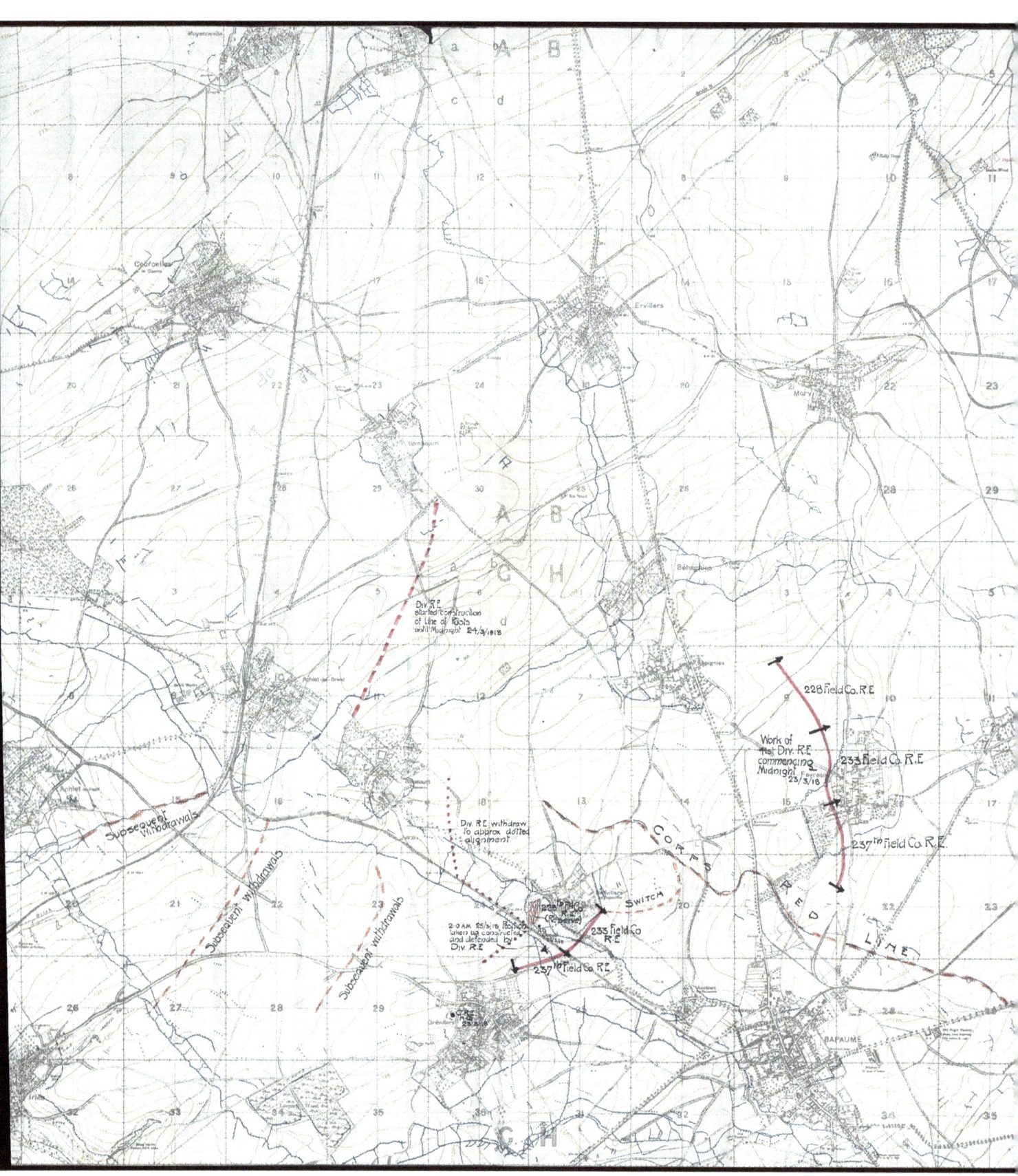

WAR DIARY

C. R. E.

41st DIVISION

APRIL 1918

ORIGINAL

Army Form C. 2118.

WAR DIARY
or
INTELLIGENCE SUMMARY.
(Erase heading not required.)

Hqrs. R.E. 41st Division

APRIL 1918

Vol 24

Place	Date	Hour	Summary of Events and Information	Remarks and references to Appendices
GAUDIEMPRE	1st		CRE (Lt. Col. En Scorley DSO) visited Hrdlays at BUCQUOY and also RE dumps being formed at HANNESCAMPS and ESSARTS. Adjutant visited 4th Corps RE dump at BUS-LES-ARTOIS. Field Coys relieved that night by 42nd Divn Engrs.	
"	2nd		Field Coys moved into Brigade Groups prior to entraining.	
"	3rd		HQRE entrained at PETIT HOUVIN. CRE & Adjutant by car to ST. OMER.	
"	4th		CRE & Adjutant visited HQRS. 2nd Army at CASSEL. HQRE returned at PESELHOEK.	
STEENWOORDE	5th		Chief Engineer II Army (Maj. Gen. Glubb) called.	
"	6th		Division was inspected by GOC VIII Corps. CRE & Adjutant visited BRANDHOEK and HQRS. VIII Corps near COUTHOVE CHATEAU	
"	7th		CRE & Adjutant visited HQRS 29th Divn. at CANAL BANK YPRES to make arrangements for taking over work on 29th Divn Sector. CRE visited Reserve Line 29th Div front.	
"	8th		CRE & Adjutant visited No 3 RE P. & R. ABEELE. 9th Corps Transport lorry at VLAMERTINGHE and VIII Corps RE P. & R. OAKHANGER	
YPRES	9th		41st Div. relieved 29th Div. HQRE moved to CANAL BANK, DEAD END, YPRES.	
"	10th		CRE & Adjutant visited 237 & 98 Coys at SOMME dugouts	

Army Form C. 2118.

WAR DIARY
or
INTELLIGENCE SUMMARY.
(Erase heading not required.)

Instructions regarding War Diaries and Intelligence Summaries are contained in F. S. Regs., Part II. and the Staff Manual respectively. Title pages will be prepared in manuscript.

APRIL 1918   HQrs. R.E. 41st Division

Place	Date	Hour	Summary of Events and Information	Remarks and references to Appendices
YPRES	12		SPREE R.E. Dump Salvage commenced and a new Dump formed at S. JEAN. 940 Coys R.E. now billeted in YPRES. Demolitions prepared in forward zone. Battle Zone occupied with outposts in front line.	
"	13		Work continued on Battle Zone	
"	14		CRE visited Army battle zone with CRE A52 (Major Hudson R.E.) In evening CRE laid out new line WIELTJE – LANCER FARM – WHITE CHATEAU (Menin Road) with Divl. Commander.	
"	15		Work commenced on WIELTJE – WHITE CHATEAU line. CRE r Divl. Commander visited this line. Adjutant visited No 3 RE Park ABEELE for explosives.	
"	16		Pulpose Rehearsed from PASCHENDAELE RIDGE. forward positions carried out by 228 & 237 940 Coys. Major W.L Shaw R.E. killed.	
"	17		CRE visited YPRES Defences	
"	18		CRE & Adjutant visited Reserve line. YPRES defences north G.O.E. 124 & Bde.	
"	19.		CRE visited Cdr Row 20 Bn (Brieken line) with GOC 122 Inf Bde.	
"	20.		CRE with GOC 123 Inf Bde, r GOC 233 Fd Coy laid out new line in left sector to include JASPER & OHLAN KEEPS.	

Army Form C. 2118.

WAR DIARY
or
INTELLIGENCE SUMMARY.
(Erase heading not required.)

H.Q.s R.E. 41st Division

APRIL 1918

Place	Date	Hour	Summary of Events and Information	Remarks and references to Appendices
YPRES	21		CRE & GSO3 visited Y/M Srebr. battle zone and also UHLAN KEEP. Afternoon CRE & Adjutant visited YPRES Defences.	
"	22		CRE & Adjutant visited Reserve dumps. 237 Fd Coy moved to SAPPER CAMP near POTIJZE. Built in YPRES Many breastworks unable owing to Gas	
"	23		Adjutant visited HOP FACTORY VLAMERTINGHE for the purpose of paying civilian labourers working there. CRE visited Rear Zone BRIELEN LINE with Capt. Thomas RE.	
"	24		CRE & Adjutant visited BRICKSPUR & light railway. Those suffer for hrs. Major Paid PR to OC 237 & 90 Coys. Evacuated to CCS suffering from effects of Gas. CRE OC Bn Durham YPRES. CRE & SOL TAKING those self for hrs. Pay H.Qs at MACHINE GUN FARM	
"	25		CRE visited 237 90 Coys at SAPPER CAMP, also Y/M Srebr. Battle Zone. H.Qrs. moved to VLAMERTINGHE Chateau and joined D.H.Q.S. 237 90 Coys moved to HOP FACTORY VLAMERTINGHE	
VLAMERTINGHE	26		233 Coy at CANAL BANK YPRES Div H.Qs moved to Don Elwood Camp POPERINGHE VD Coy transferred to 25 G BRAKE CAMP.	

Wt. W11422/M1160 355000 12/16 D.D. & L. Forms/C/2118/14.

Army Form C. 2118.

WAR DIARY
or
INTELLIGENCE SUMMARY.
(Erase heading not required.)

HQ RE 41st Div.

April 1918

Place	Date	Hour	Summary of Events and Information	Remarks and references to Appendices
POPERINGHE	27		Outposts to Dixmude to WIELTJE – WHITE CHATEAU Line. YPRES Defences reconnoitred	
" "	28		CRE visited VLAMERTINGHE Defences with Major Bateman RE & fixed junction of Green line with XXII Corps & 6th Division representative. Also visited GREEN LINE through VLAMERTINGHE with Capt Thomas RE.	
" "	29		HQ RE moved to LOVIE CHATEAU	
LOVIE Ch.	30		CRE vAd/Major visited Corps Park at ONDANK also YELLOW LINE (BRANDHOEK) and 228th Coy billets at DIRTY BUCKET CAMP.	

S M Mcoley Lt. Col. RE
CRE 41st Div.

1-5-18.

ORIGINAL

Army Form C. 2118.

H.Qrs. RE 41st Division

Vol 24

WAR DIARY
or
INTELLIGENCE SUMMARY
(Erase heading not required.)

MAY 1918

Place	Date	Hour	Summary of Events and Information	Remarks and references to Appendices
LOVIE CHATEAU	1.		CRE visited GREEN & VLAMERTINGHE LINE and YELLOW & BRANDHOEK LINE both CE II Corps.	
"	2.		Adjutant visited GREEN & YELLOW LINES also BRIELEN LINE re distribution of RE Stores to Field Coys. Working on New Tines. CE I Corps called.	
"	3.		CRE visited GREEN LINE with G.S.O.I. looked on YELLOW LINE & Co handed over to CE II Corps.	
"	4.		Adjutant visited HOPFACTORY, VLAMERTINGHE, 233rd Field Coy at YPRES, Bde. Hqrs. at ROMEFARM, Field Coy transport lines at DIRTY BUCKET CAMP and New Bde. Hqrs on YELLOW LINE	
"	6.		CRE & Adjutant visited GREEN LINE, CULLODEN SIDING, 225th Fd Coy, VLAMERTINGHE MILL, 124 Bde. Hqrs. at FOSTER CAMP.	
"	7.		CRE & Adjutant visited CE II Corps at HOUTKERQUE	
"	8.		CRE visited CRE 6th Division	
"	9.		CRE visited GREEN LINE at VLAMERTINGHE	
"	10		Adjutant visited 233rd Field Coy at YPRES with Capt. Thomas RE & an aftr relief between 225th & 233rd Field Coys.	

Army Form C. 2118.

WAR DIARY
or
INTELLIGENCE SUMMARY.
(Erase heading not required.)

HQrs. RE 41st Division

MAY 1918

Place	Date	Hour	Summary of Events and Information	Remarks and references to Appendices
LOVIE CHATEAU	11		CRE & Adjutant visited YPRES only. Defences also portion of front taken over from 6th Division. Adjutant visited CE II Corps.	
"	13		CRE visited GREEN LINE with OC 233rd Field Coy RE. Adjutant visited HQrs 122 & 124 Inf Bdes, at MACHINE GUN FARM.	
"	14		CRE visited YPRES defences. Adjutant visited No 3 RE PARK, ABEELE, also ONDANK & OAKHANGER RE. PARKS.	
"	15		CRE & Adjutant visited BRIELEN LINE and HQrs 124 Inf Bde.	
"	16		Adjutant visited CULLODEN REDUMP, GREEN LINE HQrs Miss Mermes (Roads) Headquarters at VLAMERTINGHE.	
"	17		CRE & Adjutant visited GREEN LINE with CRE Corps Troops to Precede. On Junction with his work in 6th Division area.	
"	18		CRE visited Field Corps, Transport lines.	
"	20		CRE & Adjutant visited YPRES outer Defences with CRE 124 Inf Bde, and also above line between LILLE GATE & BRIELEN LIXE RAILWAY and LILLE GATE SWITCH.	
"	21		CRE visited CRE 6th Division.	

WAR DIARY
INTELLIGENCE SUMMARY

Army Form C. 2118.

N° Dus R.E. 41st Division

MAY 1918

Place	Date	Hour	Summary of Events and Information	Remarks and references to Appendices
LOVIE	22.		CRE & Adjutant visited GREEN LINE	
CHATEAU	23.		CRE visited GREEN LINE at VLAMERTINGHE and lectured on Engineer work to Officers 8/12 = 2nd Bath E Surrey Regt. CRE & Adjutant with GSO1 visited front line in Ryhr. Palis Sector to ZILLEBEKE LAKE by night.	
"	25th		CRE visited VLAMERTINGHE and lectured to officers 8/18th Bath KRRC on field works	
"	26th		Adjutant visited 124 Inf Bde Headquarters at VLAMERTINGHE CHATEAU to arrange working parties for 233rd Road Coy on GREEN LINE. Major H.A. REID DSO, M.C. R.E. M/Divnd 40th Divn.	
"	27th		CRE visited YPRES Defences with G.S.O.1.	
"	28th		CRE visited GREEN LINE (lecture) to officers 8/25th Durham L.I.	
"	29th		Adjutant visited 228th Field Coy at YPRES	
"	30th		CRE visited GREEN LINE and lectured to officers 8/26th = R. Fusiliers	
"	31st		" " " " " " " " 10th Queens	

[signatures]
CRE R.E. 41st Divn.

Army Form C. 2118.

WAR DIARY
or
INTELLIGENCE SUMMARY.
(Erase heading not required.)

H.Qrs. R.E. 41st Division.

VR 26

Place	Date	Hour	Summary of Events and Information	Remarks and references to Appendices
	JUNE 1918			
LOVIE CHATEAU	2nd		CRE (Lt Col. F.N.Stockley) visited work in progress on "GREEN" LINE at VLAMERTINGHE	
			Adjutant (Capt. A.C.Godby) visited Field Coy. Office. Orders received for relief of	
			41st. Div. by 49th Div.	
" "	4th		HQrs. RE moved to NIEURLET. Orders received for CRE to join HQrs XIX Corps.	
			to take up appointment as Chief Engineer.	
NIEURLET	5th		CRE visited Field Coys. and Pioneer Battalion (19th Middlesex) to say	
			Good bye.	
" "	6th		Lt Col. Stockley left to take up duties of Chief Engineer XIX Corps.	
			Lt. Col. A.C. Howard M.C. R.E. joined HQ. R.E. as CRE from CRE Sqd.	
			Division.	
"	7th		CRE & Adjutant visited 233rd & 237th Field Coys. HQrs RE moved to	
			EPERLECQUES	
EPERLECQUES	8th		CRE & Adjutant visited HQrs VII Corps at HOULLES and 228th Field Coy	
			at GANSPETTE	
"	9th		CRE & Adjutant visited site for Rifle range near AUDREHEM and arranged for	
			work to commence with O.C. 237th Field Coy.	

Army Form C. 2118.

WAR DIARY
or
INTELLIGENCE SUMMARY.
(Erase heading not required.)

HQrs RE 41st Division

JUNE 1918

Place	Date	Hour	Summary of Events and Information	Remarks and references to Appendices
EPERLECQUES	10th		CRE inspected 226th Field Coy at GANSPETTE and visited 233rd Field Coy at BAYENGHEM.	
"	11th		CRE & Adjutant visited WOR by 237th Field Coy at AUDREHEM Rifle Range	
"	12th		CRE inspected 233rd Field Coy at BAYENGHEM. Visited work on AUDREHEM rifle range.	
"	14th		CRE inspected 237th Field Coy at CLERQUES	
"	16th		CRE with Adjutant & OC 19th Middlesex, visited WDR on AUDREHEM Rifle range.	
"	17th		CRE & Adjutant visited 228th Field Coy RE at GANSPETTE	
"	18th		CRE & Adjutant visited 233rd Field Coy who were taking part in a Tactical Exercise with 124th Inf Bde near TOURNEHEM.	
"	19th		CRE & Adjutant visited 237th Field Coy at CLERQUES	
"	20th		" " " 225th Field Coy at GANSPETTE	
"	21st		CRE visited WDR on AUDREHEM Rifle Range.	
"	22nd		" " 233rd Field Coy at BAYENGHEM	
"	26th		Div H.Qrs moved to DUDEZEELE	

Army Form C. 2118.

WAR DIARY
or
INTELLIGENCE SUMMARY.
(Erase heading not required.)

HQ 15 RE 41st Division

JUNE 1918

Place	Date	Hour	Summary of Events and Information	Remarks and references to Appendices
OUDEZEELE	27th		CRE visited HQrs 7th French Division near ABEELE to discuss taking over work in progress	
"	28th		CRE visited work in progress on 7th (French) Divisional Front (SCHERPENBERG sector) with C. de Genie, 7th French Div. Adjutant visited French Divisional Engineer Dump near ABEELE and made arrangements for taking it over.	
"	29th		CRE visited work being done by 7th French Division as on 28th.	
"	30th		Field Coys took over from French Engineers. CRE visited various works in progress. Adjutant arranged billets for Field Coy. transport lines near ABEELE.	

Major Capt R
for Lt Col RE
CRE 41st Division

SECRET.   Copy No. 14

ORDER NO. 1
by
C. R. E. 41 ST DIVISION.

Reference Sheet. 27.) 1.
          Sheet. 28.) 40,000.

1.   The 41st Division will relieve the 7th (French) Division on nights June 30th/July 1st and July 1st/July 2nd in the Right Division Sector of the 14th French Corps Front.
         233rd Field Coy. R.E. will relieve 4/1st Coy.
2. French Engineers on Left of Divisional Front.
         237th Field Coy. R.E. will relieve 4/51st Coy.
   French Engineers on Right of Divisional Front.
         228th Field Coy. R.E. will be in reserve.
3.   The Divisional Front will be held by 3 Brigades -
   124th Infantry Brigade on Right.
   123rd Infantry Brigade in Centre.
   122nd Infantry Brigade on Left.
         On completion of relief 237th Field Coy. R.E. will be responsible for work South West of a line G.34.b.0.2. - N.13.d.5.3. (Sheet 28).
         233rd Field Coy. R.E. will be responsible for work North-East of this line.
         19th Middlesex Regt. (Pioneers) will be responsible for construction and maintenance of Roads, Tracks and Communication Trenches on the whole of the Divisional Front.
4.   Relief will take place on night June 30th/July 1st and must be completed by 12-0 midnight.
         Billets are allotted as follows :-
   228th Field Coy. R.E. at ABEELE AERODROME.
   233rd Field Coy. R.E. (less Transport) at 4/1st French Engrs. Coy. billets at L.36.a.2.1.
   237th Field Coy. R.E. (less Transport) at 4/51st French Engrs. Coy. billets at L.36.a.2.1.
   19th Middlesex Regt (Pioneers) less transport at billets now occupied by French Territorial Battn, WIPPENHOEK.
5.   Transport of 233rd Field Coy. R.E., 237th Field Coy. R.E. and 19th Middlesex Regt (Pioneers) will billet at Sheet 27, R.2.a. & b. and L.32.d. and L.33.c.   Billeting parties for transport will report to Adjutant 41st Divl. R.E. at 11 a.m. June 30th at cross roads L.33.c.2.3.
6.   During daylight every precaution is to be taken to avoid detection by enemy aeroplane or observation balloon of a relief being in progress.
         No Movement East of the grid-line running North and South between squares G.31. and G.32. is to take place until after dark.
7.   Advance parties of 1 Officer, 2 N.C.O's and 10 O.R. will report at 9 a.m. June 30th as follows :-
                                                          Engrs)
   From 233rd Field Coy. R.E. to Headquarters 4/1st Coy. French)
   From 237th Field Coy. R.E. to H.Qrs. 4/51st Coy.French Engrs.

                                          / 8. C.R.E. Hqrs.

-2-

8. C.R.E. Headquarters will close at 7 p.m. July 1st at OUDERZEELE and re-open at the same hour at LA LINGE, L.26.a.6.7.

9. <u>ACKNOWLEDGE</u>.

R.C.Howard
Lieut.Col.R.E.
C.R.E. 41st Division.

28th June 1918.

Issued
~~Timed~~ at 9 p.m.

DISTRIBUTION.

Copy No.
1. 41st Divn. "G".
2. 41st Divn. "Q".
3. 122nd Inf.Bde.
4. 123rd Inf.Bde.
5. 124th Inf.Bde.
6. 41st Div.Train.
7. 41st Div.Sig.Coy.
8. 228th Fd.Coy.R.E.
9. 233rd Fd.Coy.R.E.
10. 237th Fd.Coy.R.E.
11. 19th Middx Regt.
12. Commdt du Genie 7e Div.
13. C.E. XIXth Corps.
14. War Diary.
15. War Diary.
16. File.

S E C R E T.

O.C. 228th Field Coy. R.E.
O.C. 233rd Field Coy. R.E.
O.C. 237th Field Coy. R.E.
C.O. 19th Middlesex Regt.
41st Division "G".   )
122nd Infantry Brigade.) For
123rd Infantry Brigade.) information.
124th Infantry Brigade.)

P R O G R A M M E   O F   W O R K.

DISPOSITIONS.   O.C. 237th Field Coy. R.E. is responsible for the Sub-Sector of the Divisional Front South West of the line G.34.b.0.2. - N.13.d.5.3.

O.C. 233rd Field Coy. R.E. is responsible for the Sub-Sector North East of this line.

O.C. 228th Field Coy. R.E. is responsible for work West of grid line between G.32. and G.33.

GENERAL.   The Battalions in the Line will be responsible for all work in the First System comprising three trenches sited forward of the main crest of the SCHERPENBERG and for the construction of a strong supporting point in each Brigade Sector.
Field Companies R.E. will give all assistance and supervision required.

The order of priority of work on these lines will be :-

FIRST SYSTEM.

(a) Wiring.
(b) Extending the present trenches to make continuous lines.
(c) Deepening and Widening and Draining.
(d) Revetting and Duckboarding.

STRONG SUPPORTING POINTS.

(a) Wiring.
(b) Digging to 3 feet throughout.
(c) Digging to depth and firestepping.
(d) Revetting and Duckboarding.

COMMUNICATION.   The Pioneer Battalion will be responsible for all Communication Trenches, Roads and Tracks.

In the first instance a communication trench giving cover from view throughout it's length must be completed on each Brigade front. Working parties will be concentrated at present on those parts of the trenches under direct observation.

/ To reduce casualties.

COMMUNICATION. (Contd).	To reduce casualties to a minimum, C.O. 19th Middlesex Regt will arrange to concentrate the whole of his available men on the forward portion of each of these trenches in turn, so that the whole length of trench under direct observation may be dug in one night.
	As soon as through communication to the Front Line is established, these trenches will be revetted and duckboarded.
REAR DEFENCES.	BRETELLE No. 1 will be put into a defensive state forthwith, also the villages of LA CLYTTE, ZEVECOTEN and RININGHELST.
DEMOLITIONS.	Work on demolitions handed over from the 7th French Division will be put in hand, subject to such modifications as have been ordered by 41st Division.
MISCELLANEOUS.	A new Headquarters for Right Brigade will be constructed by 237th Field Coy. R.E., working party from Reserve Battalion Right Brigade.
	Work on Observation Posts, Aid Posts and Road Camouflage taken over from the French will be completed.
	In addition the 228th Field Coy. R.E. in reserve will be engaged on construction of a new Divisional Headquarters and new Divisional Rest Station.
SALVAGE.	Every effort must be made to organize an efficient system of R.E. Salvage forthwith.
	No timber or corrugated Iron will be issued from Divisional Dumps.

R.C.Howard

Lieut.Col.R.E.,
C.R.E. 41st Division.

29th June 1918.

CONFIDENTIAL
98/27

WAR DIARY

of

HQRE 41st Division

JULY 1918

Army Form C. 2118.

WAR DIARY
or
INTELLIGENCE SUMMARY
(Erase heading not required.)

JULY 1918   H.Qrs. R.E. 41 Division

Place	Date	Hour	Summary of Events and Information	Remarks and references to Appendices
OUDEZEELE	1		HQrs. R.E. move to LA LINGE near ABEELE and took over GHQ 1st line defences. Headquarter Engineers, 71st French Division. CRE (Lt Col A.C. Howard M.C. R.E.) visited work taken over by Field Coys.	
LA LINGE	2		CRE visited work on Divisional Front with G.O.C. & G.S.O.1.	
Sh. 27	3		CRE visited work of 233 & 237 Field Coys with G.O.C. & G.S.O.1. 228th Field Coy proceeded work construction of Camps for new Div.l Headquarters.	
Belgium I.20.c.S.3	4		CRE visited GDR in progress with G.O.C. & G.S.O.1. Capt R. Flock (R.E.) CRE & Adjutant Capt R. Flock (R.E.) visited C.E. XIX Corps at WINNEZEELE.	
" "	5		CRE visited work of Field Coys & 19th Middlesex (Pioneers)	
" "	6		CRE & G.S.O.1. visited defence works on Divisional Front.	
" "	7		HQ.R.E. move to new Div. Headquarters near ABEELE at K.24.C.1.1. Off main ABEELE - WATOU Road. CRE & Road work in progress with G.O.C. & G.S.O.1	
K.24.C.1.1	8		ditto	
"	9		CRE visited Advanced Dressing Stations with ADMS	
"	10			

Army Form C. 2118.

WAR DIARY
or
INTELLIGENCE SUMMARY.
(Erase heading not required.)

HQrs. R.E. 41 Division

JULY 1918

Place	Date	Hour	Summary of Events and Information	Remarks and references to Appendices
K.24.C.1.1.	11		CRE visited work in Ryder Bridge & with GSO1	
Belgium St.27	12		CRE visited work in Left Bright Sector by 233 Field Coy	
			during day.	
1/40000	13		CRE visited Defence works on divisional front with GSO1	
	14		CRE & Adjutant visited Field Coy billets & HQrs 19th Div Doors	
	15		CRE & Adjutant visited Construction of Div Rest Station	
			at RWELS & 228th Field Coy.	
	16·17		CRE & GSO1 visited work of Field Coys in the line	
			with O.C.s Field Coys.	
	18		CRE visited work of 237th Field Coy with Major Butler R.E.	
	19		CRE visiting work on "Redoubt Line" & erection of huon	
			Pillboxes for M.G. Emplacements. CRE & Adjutant	
			visited R.E. dump at STEEN AKKER (L.32.d.4.0.) and	
			Field Coy billets	
" "	20		CRE visited Redoubt Line	
" "	21		CRE visited Field Coys work in the line	

WAR DIARY
INTELLIGENCE SUMMARY

Army Form C. 2118.

JULY 1918   HQrs. R.E. 4th Division

Place	Date	Hour	Summary of Events and Information	Remarks
K.24.C.1.1. Belgium	22		CRE visited work in progress on Dressing Stations & RAPs with DADMS.	
Sht 27. Y0000	23		CRE visited Erection of "Moir" Pillboxes and Construction of new Rds. HQrs. in the line by Field Corps R.E.	
"	24/25		CRE visited defence work by Field Corps.	
"	27		CE XIX Corps. called to discuss new work to be commenced and its details policy of XIX Corps etc. CRE visited Field Corps 9/19 Middlesex with Adjutant.	
"	29		CRE visited work with Field Company Commanders.	
"	30		CRE visited work of 19th Middlesex (Pioneers)	
"	31		CRE visited Field Corps R.E. and Bde. Headquarters in the line.	

Capell
Adjutant for CRE 4th Division

S E C R E T.   Copy No........

OPERATION ORDER NO. 2.

BY C.R.E. 41ST DIVISION.

Reference Sheet 28. 1/40,000.
KEMMEL 1/10,000.
POPERINGHE 1/10,000.

1.   On night July 15/16th the following reliefs will take place :-

   (a)   228th Field Coy. R.E. will take over work in Right Sub-Sector from 237th Field Coy. R.E.

   (b)   237th Field Coy. R.E. will take over all work in Centre Sub-Sector from 233rd Field Coy. R.E.

2.   The greatest care is to be taken that all details of work in progress are handed over to ensure continuity of work.

3.   228th Field Coy. R.E. will move to billets and bivouacs already selected in M.2.a., wagon lines remaining at 27/L.25.b.5.7.

4.   Relief to be completed by 3 a.m. 16th inst.

5.   ACKNOWLEDGE.

                                                Lieut.Col.D.T.,
14th July 1918.   C.R.E. 41st Division.

Copy No.1. 228th Fd. Coy. R.E.   9. 124th Inf.Bde.
        2. 233rd Fd. Coy. R.E.   10. O.C. Div Train.
        3. 237th Fd. Coy. R.E.   11. A.D.M.S.
        4. 19th Bn.Middlesex Rgt. 12. D.A.D.O.S.
        5. 41st Division "G"   13. 41st Div.Sig.Coy.
        6. 41st Division " "   14. C.E. XIXth Corps.
        7. 122nd Inf.Bde.   15. Office.
        8. 123rd Inf.Bde.   16 & 17. War Diary.

WAR DIARY
or
INTELLIGENCE SUMMARY.

(Erase heading not required.)

Army Form C. 2118.

H.Qrs. R.E. 41st Division   Vol 28

AUGUST 1918

Place	Date	Hour	Summary of Events and Information	Remarks and references to Appendices
K.24.c.1.1. Belgium Sht. 27. 1/40000	1st		CRE (Lt Col. A.C. Howard M.C. R.E.) visited work of Field Coys in the line and also made arrangements for taking over work of 233rd Field Coy by 228th + 237th Field Coys.	
"	2nd		CRE visited 228th + 237th Field Coys. Adjutant (Capt A. McClosky '19) visited No 5 Forway Coy R.E. to arrange for Reus Spurs to be built for the purpose of stacking Reus forward R.E. dumps.	
"	3		CRE visited work of 228th Field Coy on WESTOUTRE Line.	
"	4		CRE visited 233rd Field Coy who had moved on the 2nd inst to HELFAUT for training.	
"	5		Adjutant visited Field Coys and Div R.E. Dumps. CRE visited work on dressing stations and RAPs with DADMS.	
"	6		CRE visited H.Qrs XIXCorps at WINNEZEELE on the occasion of the visit of H.M. the King. CRE attended Conference of Div & Brigade Commanders at H.Qrs. 123rd Infantry Brigade.	
"	7		CRE visited Divisional Rest Station at RWFW. CRE and Adjutant visited Field Coys. 233rd Coy returned from HELFAUT	

Army Form C. 2118.

WAR DIARY
or
INTELLIGENCE SUMMARY.
(Erase heading not required.)

H.Qrs. R.E. 41st Division

AUGUST 1918

Place	Date	Hour	Summary of Events and Information	Remarks and references to Appendices
K24C.1.1.	8.		CRE visited work in progress on Divl front and also H.Qrs of each infantry Bde. 233 Field Coy took part in successful minor operation on left of Divl front in conjunction with 15th Batt. Hampshire Regt.	
Belgium Sheet 27 V.40000	9.		CRE visited Field Corps. billets	
"	10.		CRE inspected work on WESTOUTRE LINE with G.S.O.1.	
"	11.		CRE visited Field Coy billets to arrange for relief of 233rd Field Coy by 237th Field Coy	
"	12.		CRE visited H.Qrs. Inf. Bdes. in the line and inspected work in progress on Divisional front	
"	13.		CRE visited H.Qrs. left Brigade in the line and inspected works in progress in that Sector	
"	14.		CRE visited Field Coys and also defence work on the WESTOUTRE Line	
"	15.		CRE visited Divnl Rsol. Station, inspected tunnelling work in progress	
"	16.		CRE & Adjutant visited H.Qrs left Flank Bdes in the line and field Coy billets.	

Army Form C. 2118.

WAR DIARY
or
INTELLIGENCE SUMMARY.
(Erase heading not required.)

Hqrs RE Division

AUGUST 1918

Place	Date	Hour	Summary of Events and Information	Remarks and references to Appendices
K24 C.I.I.	17		CRE visited 124th Inf Bde sector and SCHERPENBURG defences	
Belgium	18		CRE visited HQrs Inf Bde in the line and inspected	
Sheet 27			WoR on SCHERPENBERG - DICKEBUSCH LAKE line	
Voodoo	19		CRE visited Field Coys RE - "Loose" line	
	21		CRE visited WoR on C.T.S. in Divisional Sector. CRE & Adjutant	
			visited CE XIX Corps re schemes for proposed WoR. CRE will a	
			Conference of Field Coy. Commanders at Div. H.Qrs.	
	22		CRE visited WoR in Centre Brigade Sector. Adjutant	
			visited XIX Corps Headquarters.	
	23		CRE visited WoR on Communication in progress by 19th Bn.	
			Middlesex (Pioneers)	
	24		CRE visited WoR on RAPs & strong stations WoR DADMS	
	26		CRE visited WoR to procure on left Bgd front with CSOI.	
			CRE visited H.Qrs. XIX Corps at WINNEZEELE	
	27		CRE visited LOVIE CHATEAU to discuss certain details of WoR by CRE	
			34th Division	

Army Form C. 2118.

WAR DIARY
or
INTELLIGENCE SUMMARY. H. Qrs. R.E. 41 Division
(Erase heading not required.)

AUGUST 1918

Place	Date	Hour	Summary of Events and Information	Remarks and references to Appendices
K.24.c.1.1. Belgium Sht 27.V 40.000	28.		CRE visited work on Div^l Front with CRE 34th Division with a view to handing over. Adjutant handed over Div^l Dump & Workshops to Adjutant R.E. 34th Division	
	29.		H.Qrs. R.E. moved to WIZERNES. CRE remained with CRE 34th Division in order to hand over details & stores to CRE 34th Division properly.	
WIZERNES	30.		CRE rejoined H.Qrs. R.E. and visited 233rd Fied Coy R.E. at HALLINES	
	31.		CRE visited 237 Fied Coy R.E. in billets at LONGUENESSE	

[signature]
A. Horn Capt R.E.
A/W for Lt. Col. R.E.
CRE 41st Divn

SECRET.

Copy No.........

OPERATION ORDER NO. 6

by

C. R. E. 41st DIVISION.

Reference Maps:-
KEMMEL, POPERINGHE 1/10,000
HAZEBROUCK 5 A. 1/100,000.

27th August 1918.

1. The 41st Division (less Artillery) will be relieved by 34th Division (less Artillery and one Infantry Brigade and plus 18th Infantry Brigade 6th Division) beginning on night August 28th/29th.

2. The relief of Field Companies R.E., and Pioneer Battalion will be as follows:-
    (a) On night August 28th/29th 207th Field Co R.E. will take over billets of 233rd Field Co R.E.,
    (b) On night August 29th/30th 207th Field Co R.E., will relieve 237th Field Co R.E., in 123rd Infantry Brigade Sector. Relief to be completed by 12 midnight.
    (c) On night August 29th/30th 208th Field Co R.E. will take over billets of 237th Field Co R.E., and all work in rear of Redoubt Line on the Divisional Front. Relief to be completed by 12 midnight.
    (d) On night August 29th/30th 209th Field Co R.E., will take over work in 124th Infantry Brigade Sector and billets of 228th Field Co R.E.
    Relief to be completed by 12 midnight.
    (e) On night August 29th/30th, 2nd/4th Somerset Light Infantry(Pioneers) will take over work and billets of 19th Battn Middlesex Regt(Pioneers) on Divisional Front.

3. On completion of reliefs 233rd Field Co R.E., will entrain with 122nd Infantry Brigade for ESQUERDES.
237th Field Co R.E., will entrain with 123rd Infantry Brigade for ST MARTIN-AU-LAERT.
Further orders will be issued for disposal of 228th Field Co.R.E., and 19th Battn Middlesex Regt(Pioneers).

4. Full statements of all work proposed and in hand will be handed over to relieving units and a copy of such statements forwarded to this Office.
   All Defence Schemes, Aeroplane Photos, Trench Stores, Anti-Aircraft Posts etc, will be handed over on relief.
   Lists of R.E. Stores in Forward Dumps will be handed over and receipts obtained.

5. Advanced Parties of one Officer and four N.C.Os from 34th Division will report to each Field Co R.E., and Pioneer Battalion on August 28th.

.2.

.6. Officers commanding Field Companies R.E., and 19th Battn Middlesex Regt(Pioneers,) will arrange to leave behind one Officer per Field Co R.E., and one Officer from each Company of 19th Battn Middlesex Regt(Pioneers) for 24 hours after the completion of their respective reliefs.

.7. ACKNOWLEDGE.

Issued out 6 p.m.

Lieut.Colonel R.E.,
C.R.E.,41st Division.

DISTRIBUTION.

Copy No.	
1.	41st Division "G"
2.	41st " "A"
3.	C.R.A.
4.	122rd Infantry Brigade.
5.	123rd " "
6.	124th " "
7.	228th Field Co R.E.
8.	233rd " " "
9.	237th " " "
10.	19th Battn Middlesex Regt(Pioneers)
11.	A.D.M.S.
12.	41st Divisional Train.
13.	41st Divisional Signal Co R.E.
14.	D.A.D.O.S.
15.	D.A.D.V.S.
16.	A.P.M.
17.	C.E.,19th Corps.
18.	C.R.E., 34th Division.
19.	War Diary.
20.	War Diary.
21.	Office.

SECRET.   Copy No. 10

OPERATION ORDER NO. 5

by

C.R.E. 41ST DIVISION.

Reference Maps:-
POPERINGHE.)
KEMMEL.   ) 1/10,000.   15th August 1918.

1.-   On the night 17th/18th August 1918 the
following reliefs will take place :-

   (a) 233rd Field Coy. R.E. will relieve 237th
       Field Coy. R.E. in the Left Brigade Sector.

       237th Field Coy. R.E. will relieve 228th
       Field Coy. R.E. in the Centre Brigade Sector.

   (b) 233rd Field Coy. R.E. will take over from
       228th Field Coy. R.E. all work on R.A.P's
       and A.D.S's in Left Brigade Sector

2.-   O.C. 228th Field Coy. R.E. will retain
responsibility for the WESTOUTRE - GOED MOET MILL
LINE throughout the Divisional Front.

3.-   ACKNOWLEDGE.

                                      R.A.J.Howard

                                 Lieut. Col. R.E.,
                              C.R.E. 41st Division.

DISTRIBUTION.

Copy No. 1. 41st Divn. "G"   6. 123 Inf. Bde.
         2. 228 Fd. Coy. R.E.   7. 124 Inf. Bde.
         3. 233 Fd. Coy. R.E.   8. A.D.M.S.
         4. 237 Fd. Coy. R.E.   9. War Diary.
         5. 122 Inf. Bde.   10. War Diary.

SECRET.   Copy No. 10

OPERATION ORDER No. 4.

BY

C.R.E. 41ST DIVISION.   11th August 1918.

Reference Maps:-
KEMMEL.   )
POPERINGHE.) 1/10,000.

On the night August 11th/12th the following reliefs will take place :-

(a) 237th Field Coy. R.E. will be placed at the disposal of the G.O.C. 123rd Infantry Brigade for consolidation work in Left Brigade Sector, relieving 233rd Field Coy. R.E.

(b) On relief, 233rd Field Coy. R.E. will withdraw to billets to re-organize.

(c) 229th Field Coy. R.E. will place 1 Officer and 6 other ranks at the disposal of the G.O.C. 123rd Infantry Brigade for R.E. work forward of the REDOUBT LINE.

(d) 228th Field Coy. R.E. will be responsible for work on WESTOUTRE- GOED MORT MILL LINE throughout the Divisional Front.

ACKNOWLEDGE.

Lieut. Col. R.E.,
C.R.E. 41st Division.

Copy No. 1. 41st Divn. "G"   6. 123rd Inf. Bde.
        2. 228th Fd. Coy. R.E.   7. 124th Inf. Bde.
        3. 233rd Fd. Coy. R.E.   8. A.D.M.S.
        4. 237th Fd. Coy. R.E.   9. War Diary.
        5. 122nd Inf. Bde.   10. War Diary.

SECRET.   Copy No. 17

OPERATION ORDER NO. 3

by

C.R.E. 41ST DIVISION.   1st August 1918.

Reference Maps - Sheet 28. 1/40,000.
               HAZEBROUCK 5a. 1/100,000.

1.- 233rd Field Coy. R.E. will be withdrawn from the line on August 2nd 1918 and will move by lorry to HELFAUT and BILQUES under arrangement as laid down in 41st Division Administrative Instruction No. 37 dated 1-8-1918.

2.- In consequence of the withdrawal of the 233rd Field Coy. R.E. the following re-arrangements of work will take place from the 2nd instant inclusive:-

O.C. 228th Field Coy. R.E. will retain responsibility for work in Right Brigade Sub-Sector and will take over WESTOUTRE-GOED MOET MILL LINE throughout the Divisional Front and all work in rear of this line now being carried out by the 233rd Field Coy. R.E.

O.C. 237th Field Coy. R.E. will take over all work in Left Brigade Sub-Sector forward of the WESTOUTRE-GOED MOET MILL LINE from 233rd Field Coy. R.E.

O.C. 237th Field Coy. R.E. will hand over to 228th Field Coy. R.E. all work on the WESTOUTRE-GOED MOET MILL LINE.

3.- All details of handing over will be arranged by O's C. Field Coys. concerned.

4.- On the 2nd inst. a detachment of 500 o.r. XIXth Corps Reinforcement Battn will be at the disposal of the O.C. 228th Field Coy. R.E. for work on the WESTOUTRE-GOED MOET MILL LINE.

5.- The Platoon of American Engineers now attached to 233rd Field Coy. R.E. will be transferred to 237th Field Coy R.E. for attachment.

6.- ACKNOWLEDGE.

R C Howard
Lieut.Col.R.E.,
C.R.E. 41st Division.

Copy No. 1. 228 Fd.Coy.R.E.   10. O.C. Signals, 41 Div.
         2. 235 Fd.Coy.R.E.   11. O.C. 41st Div.Train.
         3. 237 Fd.Coy.R.E.   12. 41st Bn. M.G.C.
         4. 41st Divn."G".   13. C.E. XIXth Corps.
         5. 41st Divn."Q".   14. 102nd Engrs.27th Am.Div.
         6. 122 Inf. Bde.   15. Office.
         7. 123 Inf. Bde.   16. War Diary.
         8. 124 Inf. Bde.   17. War Diary.
         9. A.D.M.S.

CONFIDENTIAL

Vol 29

War Diary
at
H.Q.R.E. 41st Division

SEPTEMBER 1918

Army Form C. 2118.

WAR DIARY
or
INTELLIGENCE SUMMARY.
(Erase heading not required.)

H.Qrs R.E. 41 Division.

SEPTEMBER 1918

Instructions regarding War Diaries and Intelligence Summaries are contained in F. S. Regs., Part II. and the Staff Manual respectively. Title pages will be prepared in manuscript.

Place	Date	Hour	Summary of Events and Information	Remarks and references to Appendices
WIZERNES	1		C.R.E. visited 27th Amer. Div. & discussed taking over. (Lt. Col Howard M.S. R.E.)	
	2		C.R.E. visited 228th Field Co. R.E. at rein billets (Gise 53.50) Adjutant (Capt Flower) proceeded to U.K. on leave.	
	3		41st Div. took over from 27th Amer. Div. H.Qrs R.E. moved to (Sketch) L.14.a.20 C.R.E. visited Field Coys billets + 19th Middlesex (Pioneers) and reconnoitred roads around DICKEBUSCH, RIDGE WOOD + BRASSERIE.	
DOUGLAS. CAMP L.14.a.20 Belgium Sheet 27.	4		C.R.E. visited Field Coys + 19th Middlesex (Pioneers), also roads around VIERSTRAAT.	
	5		C.R.E. visited VIERSTRAAT, BRASSERIE & SCOTTISH WOOD with A.D.M.S. C.E. XIX Corps called.	
	6		C.R.E. visited DICKEBUSCH, VIERSTRAAT + line of resistance. C.R.E. visited C.E. XIX Corps.	
	7		C.R.E. visited sight for new Divisional H.Q. with A.A. Q.M.G., 123 Bde H.Q. and work at DICKEBUSCH KACK and VIERSTRAAT. C.R.E. visited C.E. XIX Corps to discuss work on new Div H.Q.	
	8		C.R.E. reconnoitred 1st, 2nd + 3rd lines of the SCHERPENBERG — DICKE-BUSCH LAKE LINE and visited advanced dressing stations at VIVYERHOEK.	

Army Form C. 2118.

WAR DIARY
or
INTELLIGENCE SUMMARY.
(Erase heading not required.)

H. QRS. R.E. 41st Division

SEPTEMBER 1918

Instructions regarding War Diaries and Intelligence Summaries are contained in F. S. Regs., Part II. and the Staff Manual respectively. Title pages will be prepared in manuscript.

Place	Date	Hour	Summary of Events and Information	Remarks and references to Appendices
DOUGLAS CAMP L.H.Q. 20. Belgium Sht 27	8		DICKEBUSCH LAITERIE, Long Barn, and Walking Wounded Post	
			C.R.E visited 222nd + 237th Fd Coys	
	9		C.R.E visited new D.H.Q (28/9 19611.) and the New Field Coys.	
	10		C.R.E attended Divisional Commander's conference at 123 Bde H.Q visited Long Barn A.D.S, VIERSTRAAT Cross Roads, BRASSERIE RIDGE and VIJVERHOEK A.D.S. C.R.E. held a conference of Field Coy Commanders at 228th Wagon lines.	
	11		C.R.E visited C.O. 19th Middlesex (P) and the 222nd + 237th Field Coys.	
	12		C.R.E. with G.S.O.2 visited 123+124 Inf Bde H.Q and work in Scottish Wood + VIERSTRAAT Switch. C.R.E. visited 233rd Field Coy	
	13		C.R.E. visited Scottish Wood, VIERSTRAAT SWITCH, VIJVERHOEK A.D.S. and Long Barn A.D.S, and 237th Field Coy R.E.	
	14		C.R.E visited Divisional Baths, Long Barn A.D.S, the New Field Coys 4123 Bde H.Q	
	15		C.R.E visited work on New Divisional H.Q, Long Barn A.D.S, the New Field Coy Commanders and 123 Bde H.Q. C.R.E. visited C.E. x Corps and new	

Army Form C. 2118.

WAR DIARY
or
INTELLIGENCE SUMMARY.
(Erase heading not required.)

H.Q.R.S. R.E. 41st DIVISION

SEPTEMBER 1918

Instructions regarding War Diaries and Intelligence Summaries are contained in F. S. Regs., Part II. and the Staff Manual respectively. Title pages will be prepared in manuscript.

Place	Date	Hour	Summary of Events and Information	Remarks and references to Appendices
DOUGLAS CAMP Nr O.30 Belgium Sheet 27	15		Area work. Bde Major 123 Bde.	
	16		C.R.E. visited 123 Bde H.Q., 16th Rwy Field Coys, and work on LONG BARN A.D.S. and new signal test box.	
	17		Adjutant (Capt. A.S. GLOVER R.E.) returned after leave to U.K.	
	18		C.R.E. & Adjutant visited VIERSTRAAT, HALLEBAST R.E. dump and Field Coys billets near OUDERDOM.	
	19		C.R.E. visited RENINGHELST area with A.A. & Q.M.G. to inspect billeting accommodation for Force Corps R.E.	
	20		C.R.E. visited Field Coys in their new billets & also attended Div. Commanders conference. C.R.E's 14th & 34th Divisions called to discuss proposed work.	
	21		C.R.E. & Adjutant visited C.E. XIX Corps at WINNEZEELE.	
	22		C.R.E. attended Div. Commanders conference and visited field Coys R.E. at their billets. C.R.E. & Adjutant visited C.R.E. 14th Division.	
	23		Adjutant visited C.R.E. 14th Divn. also XIX Corps R.E. Park BUSSEBOOM, also site of new Corps dump at DEN GROENEN JAGER CABT. C.R.E. visited R.E. Park Coys &c.	

Army Form C. 2118.

WAR DIARY
or
INTELLIGENCE SUMMARY.
(Erase heading not required.)

HQrs RE 41st Division

Place	Date	Hour	Summary of Events and Information	Remarks and references to Appendices
DOUGLAS CAMP	23		and also Site of proposed Causeways across the YPRES – COMINES CANAL near LANKHOF CHATEAU which 228th Fd Coy commenced work that night.	
L.14.a.2.0	24		CRE visited Field Coys and 19th Middlesex (Purs.)	
Belgium Sh.27	25		CRE visited Field Coys and 19th Middlesex (Purs.)	
1/40000	26		CRE and Adjutant visited Advanced Div. HQrs at MERSEY CROSS, advanced XIX Corps HQ dump at DEN GROENEN JAGER CAB.I. and held a Conference of Field Coy Commanders and O.C. 19th Middlesex (Purs.) at HQrs 228th Field Coy R.E.	
	27.		HQrs RE moved to Advanced Div. HQrs. at MERSEY CROSS near OUDERDOM. CRE visited Fd Coys who were in BRANDHOEK AREA.	
MERSEY CROSS Belgium Sh. 28.G.23.c.7.5.	28		XIX Corps attacked. Field Corps proceeded to work on forward roads. CRE visited their work and also ??? situation as far as BATTLE WOOD.	
1/40000	29		CRE visited Corps at work on WERBRANDENMOLEN – HOLLEBEKE road and reconnoitred roads & bridges at HOUTHEM and KORTEWILDE. H.Q.s. RE moved with Advanced D.H.Q. to neighbourhood of LOCK 8. T.32.a.9.5.	
LOCK 8. T.32.a.9.5.	30		CRE visited Fd Coys at work as on 29th inst. on forward and reconnoitred HOUTHEM and COMINES	

R. Sprason Capt RE
Adjutant for C.R.E. 41st Divn.

WAR DIARY
or
INTELLIGENCE SUMMARY

Army Form C. 2118.

H.Qrs. R.E. 41st Division

OCTOBER 1918

Place	Date	Hour	Summary of Events and Information	Remarks and references to Appendices
FORT GARRY Q^t Belgium 10 Sheet 28 1/40000 J.13.d.9.9/2	10		CRE visited work of field coys on forward roads	
	11		CRE made reconnaissance of roads in neighbourhood of GHELUWE	
	12		CRE visited work on ZANDVOORD-wervicq Road. CRE & O.C. 19th Middx. (Pioneers) visited work on roads near ZANDVOORD and KRUISEECKE	
	13		CRE visited field coys. CRE held conference of field coy commanders and O.C. 19th Middlesex (Pnrs).	
	14		41st Div attacked on GHELUVE front. Good progress on roads. Field coys & Pioneers on roads except 233 Field Coy which stood by ready to attempt the bridging of the RIVER LYS should the situation be favourable.	
	15		CRE visited field coys. Bridging operations were not carried out. Warning order received for 41st Div. to relieve 36th Divⁿ.	
	16		CRE visited H.Qrs. 36th Division near LEDEGHEM. H.Qrs RE moved with Div H.Qrs to ASHMORE FARM near MOORSEELE.	

Army Form C. 2118.

WAR DIARY
or
INTELLIGENCE SUMMARY.
(Erase heading not required.)

H.Qrs. R.E. 41st Division

OCTOBER 1918

Place	Date	Hour	Summary of Events and Information	Remarks and references to Appendices
ASHMORE FARM	17		CRE reconnoitred RIVER LYS at Courtrai	
Belgium Sht 28 A.1000	18		CRE visited COURTRAI with O.C. Field Coys. to reconnoitre for suitable sites for bridging the RIVER LYS.	
L.15.C.9.0	19		CRE visited CRE 35th Division & Bgde H.Qrs. 233rd & 237th Field Coys RE placed at disposal of CRE 35th Division. CRE visited 228th Coy RE during construction of foot bridge over RIVER LYS at COURTRAI.	
	20		CRE & Adjutant visited field coys. engaged on roads & bridging at BISSEGHEM. H.Qrs. Bgde. moved to POESELHOEK near GULLEGHEM.	
POESELHOEK Belgium Sht 29 A.4000 G.22.C.3.6.	21		CRE visited 228th Field Coy RE engaged in ferrying Heavy Artillery across R. LYS at BISSEGHEM by means of a raft built on 2 barges. Adjutant visited 228th Field. Advanced CRE's H.Qrs. moved to HOOGHE, Sht. 29. N.9.6.15.15. CRE visited 233rd & 237th Field Coys who were detailed to make crossings on the COURTRAI–BOSSUYT CANAL to enable attacking brigades (122nd & 124th Infy Bdes) to pass over.	
HOOGHE N.9.6.15.15	22		CRE visited Field Coys, also Gridge erected by 233 – Bgles Coy RE on COURTRAI – BOSSUYT CANAL near KNOKKE.	

Army Form C. 2118.

WAR DIARY
or
INTELLIGENCE SUMMARY.
(Erase heading not required.)

HQrs. RE. 41st Division

OCTOBER 1918

Place	Date	Hour	Summary of Events and Information	Remarks and references to Appendices
HOOGHE	23		CRE visited 233rd & 237th Field Coys, affiliated to 123 - 124 - Inf.	
Belgium			Brigades during operations. Slight progress made in advance towards R. SCHELDT.	
Sh. 29 N.9.6.15-24	24		CRE visited Capt. Deverry, dump of Engineers Stores captured at KROKKE. Large quantities of timber yet kinds found to be available for intended bridging operations on the SCHELDT 233rd Field Coy R.E. placed in charge of all the Divisional Bridging Equipment and Pontoon which were parked at SWEVERGHEM.	
	25		CRE visited Field Coys.	
	26		CRE visited 19th Middlesex (P) at work on road between LE CHAT CAST. and KAPELLE MILAENE. Also on bridges at MARCKE.	
	27		CRE & Adjutant visited HQrs 19th Middlesex at MARCKE. HQrs RE moved to farm at N.10.c.2.7 (HOOGMAN FOEY)	
HOOGMAN FOEY	28.		CRE visited R.Lys abov. COURTRAI with 2nd/Lt. Coy Commanders.	
N.10.c.2.7			Companies commenced training Rapid Bridging & making of Floating Bridges.	

Army Form C. 2118.

WAR DIARY
or
INTELLIGENCE SUMMARY.
(Erase heading not required.)

H.Qrs. R.E. 41st Division.

Place	Date	Hour	Summary of Events and Information	Remarks and references to Appendices
HOOGMAN FOEY	30.		Adjutant visited Field Coy re bridging practice on R. LYS, COURTRAI	
Belgium Sh.29	31.		CRE visited Field Coys pontooning on R. LYS and also 237th Field Coy billets. Adjutant visited 25th Field Coy billets	
40.000 N.10.c.9.7.				

Bjarne Capt R.E.
Adj. for Lt. Col. R.E., C.R.E. in Div.

WR 31

CONFIDENTIAL

WAR DIARY
of
Headquarters RE
— 41st DIVISION —

NOVEMBER 1918.

Army Form C. 2118.

WAR DIARY
or
INTELLIGENCE SUMMARY.
(Erase heading not required.)

HQrs. R.E. 41 Division

NOVEMBER 1918

Instructions regarding War Diaries and Intelligence Summaries are contained in F. S. Regs., Part II. and the Staff Manual respectively. Title pages will be prepared in manuscript.

Place	Date	Hour	Summary of Events and Information	Remarks and references to Appendices
HOOGMAN FOEY Belgium Shr.29} 1/40000 N.16.c.27.	1.		CRE visited Field Coys. at Bridging Practice on R.LYS at COURTRAI.	
	2.		CRE visited Field Coys. who continued training both with pontoons and floating Bridges on LYS at COURTRAI Div. Headquarters moved to ST. LOUIS.	
ST. LOUIS T.34.d.9.7.	3		CRE visited Field Coys. at COURTRAI. Adjutant visited Enemy Refugee Park near STEENBRUGGE taken over by C.E. XIX Corps. New CE II Corps.	
"	4.		CRE. (Lt.Col. A.C. HOWARD M.C.B.) inspected floating Bridges on R.LYS. made by Field Coys., also visited CE XIX Corps at POTTLEBERG.	
"	5.		CRE held Conference with Field Coy Commanders and C.O 19th Bath Middlesex Regt. (Pioneers) to discuss intended crossing of RIVER SCHELDT near BERCHEM.	
"	6.		CRE attended Divisional Commanders Conference at H.Qrs. 124 Infy Bde. VICHTE CHATEAU	

Army Form C. 2118.

WAR DIARY
or
INTELLIGENCE SUMMARY.
(Erase heading not required.)

HQrs RE 41 Division

NOVEMBER 1918

Place	Date	Hour	Summary of Events and Information	Remarks and references to Appendices
ST LOUIS I.34.d.9.7.	7		CRE visited Field Corps RE. HQrs RE moved to VICHTE Sch.	
VICHTE	8		Divisional Headquarters. CRE visited Field Corps billeted in ANSEGHEM area. Orderlies (Cpl HASTINGS Rt) visited XIX Corps RE Park near STEENBRUGGE. Orders W3Re received at 23.15 that patrols reported E. bank of R. SCHELDT clear of enemy and crossing of bridges would be thrown across as quickly as possible. Field Coys thereafter put out: 0700 8 floating footbridges & 1 medium pontoon bridge closing early hours of 9th inst.	
"	9		CRE visited Bridges etc, put across R. SCHELDT during night 8th/9th by Field Coys.	
"	10		HQrs RE moved to CASTER with D.H.Qrs. CRE departed on 14 days leave to U.K. It. Col HAREID DSO MC (Commanding 19th Bn. Middlesex Rgt) took up duties of acting CRE.	
CASTER	11		Hostilities ceased at 11.00 Div HQrs moved to SCHOORISSE HQrs RE billeted at Sh. 36. M.24. C.O.O. BOSCHGAT.	
BOSCHGAT	12		HQrs RE moved to NEDERBRAKEL. CRE visited Field Coys.	

Army Form C. 2118.

WAR DIARY
or
INTELLIGENCE SUMMARY.

(Erase heading not required.)

NOVEMBER 1918   H.Q. is R.E. 41 Div^n

Instructions regarding War Diaries and Intelligence Summaries are contained in F. S. Regs., Part II, and the Staff Manual respectively. Title pages will be prepared in manuscript.

Place	Date	Hour	Summary of Events and Information	Remarks and references to Appendices
NEDERBRAKEL	13		CRE & Adjutant visited Field Coy & Pioneer Battalion still employed on roads in valleys of SCHELDT near BERCHEM.	
"	14		CRE visited Field Coys & Pioneer Battalion in billets at OPBRAKEL & BOSCHSTRAAT on their arrival	
"	15		CRE attended Divl Commanders Conference. Arrangements for march to Germany were discussed.	
"	16		CRE visited Pioneer Battalion (19th Middlesex) & Field Coys	
"	17.		RE with Adjutant	
"	18.		CRE attended Thanksgiving service in NEDERBRAKEL Church. March into Germany commenced by II Corps. 41 Div on left of Corps front. 29th Div on right. HQrs moved to SANTBERGEN	
SANTBERGEN	19		CRE & Adjutant visited site of German trenches on NINOVE - HAL road manned by Field Coys R.E.	
"	21.		127 German Anti aircraft guns found by Field Coys R.E. Orders received that march would not be continued until further orders. H.Qrs. RE moved to GRAMMONT with Divl HQrs.	
GRAMMONT	22		CRE & Adjutant visited BRUSSELS	

Army Form C. 2118.

WAR DIARY or INTELLIGENCE SUMMARY.

(Erase heading not required.)

NOVEMBER 1918
H.Qrs. R.E. 41st Division

Place	Date	Hour	Summary of Events and Information	Remarks and references to Appendices
GRAMMONT	24		CRE & Adjutant visited 19th Batt Middlesex Regt (Pnrs) IDEGHEM	
"	25		Adjutant visited Pioneer Battalion HQrs (DEGHEM & ALLEW?)ED Conference to discuss Intale Divisional football Competition	
"	26		CRE (Lt Col R.C. Howard M.C. R.E.) returned from leave U.K.	
"	27		Lt Col H.A. Reid DSO M.C. left to resume duties as CD	
"	28		19th Batt Middlesex (Pnrs) from acting CRE. CRE visited field Coys RE	
"	29		CRE inspected field Corp RE at their billets	
"	30		CRE attended Divisional Commanders Conference on Athletics and Recreation during the coming winter.	

Asyton Capt & R.E.
Adjutant for CRE 41st Div"

CONFIDENTIAL.
WA 32

WAR DIARY

of

HEADQUARTERS RE 4th DIVISION

for

DECEMBER 1918

WAR DIARY or INTELLIGENCE SUMMARY

Army Form C. 2118.

HQrs RE 41st Division

DECEMBER 1918

Place	Date	Hour	Summary of Events and Information	Remarks and references to Appendices
GRAMMONT	1		CRE (Lt Col A.C. Howard MC) visited Field Coys	
"	3		CRE visited Field Coys RE	
"	6		CRE & Adjutant (Capt A.S. Glover RE) attended inspection of Field Coys RE by Divisional Commander Maj. Gen. Sir S.B. Lawford KCB	
"	7		CRE visited 233 & Field Coy RE at HERTHOUT. (TOURNAI 1.S. 100000)	
"	9		CRE visited 233 Field Coy RE	
"	10		CRE visited 225th Field Coy RE	
"	11		CRE & Adjutant attended Divisional Commanders parade for promulgation of French Decorations. CRE received Croix de Guerre à l'ordre du Corps. Adjutant received Croix de Guerre à l'ordre de Division.	
"	12		Div. l H.Qrs. Move to ENGHIEN on resumption of march to GERMANY	
ENGHIEN	13		Move to HAL	
HAL	14		Move to BRAINE L'ALLEUD	
BRAINE L'ALLEUD	17		Move to MARBAIS	

WAR DIARY or INTELLIGENCE SUMMARY

Army Form C. 2118.

H.Qrs. R.E. 41st Division

DECEMBER 1918

Place	Date	Hour	Summary of Events and Information	Remarks and references to Appendices
MARBAIS	18		Divisional HQrs. moved to MAZY	
MAZY	19		" " " " WARET LA CHAUSSÉE	
WARET LA CHAUSSÉE	20		" " " " VINALMONT. Adjutant visited	
VINALMONT	21		MOHA and arranged billets for Field Corps R.E. CRE visited MOHA & inspected billets of Field Corps R.E. Chief Engineer I Corps (Brig Genl Boileau) called.	
" "	22		CRE visited site of proposed rifle range near HUY with G.S.O. 2. Adjutant visited HUY in search of lumber	
" "	23		CRE visited site of proposed rifle range with Lt 237 Field Coy R.E.	
" "	24		CRE visited Field Corps at MOHA. Adjutant visited 432 & 433 Field Coy R.E. at HUY arranged to draw enemy limber found by them. CRE & Adjutant visited HQrs. I Corps at ANDENNE	
" "	25		CRE visited Field Corps R.E. at MOHA	
" "	26		Adjutant attended conference at DHQ with reference to proposed 4:45 Army Horse Show.	
" "	27		CRE visited Field Corps R.E. at MOHA	

Army Form C. 2118.

WAR DIARY
or
INTELLIGENCE SUMMARY.
(Erase heading not required.)

HQrs RE 41st Division

DECEMBER 1918

Place	Date	Hour	Summary of Events and Information	Remarks and references to Appendices
VINALMONT	29.		CRE visited 231st Coys RE at MOHA. (Capt G.O'Connell M.C. RAMC) Medical Officer t/o RE left for duty in England 3.O.R.	
	31.		O/HQrs RE, 41st Division left unit for Demobilisation.	

J.Parr. Capt RE
for Lt Col RE
Adjutant for CRE RE
CRE 41st Division

CONFIDENTIAL

Vol 33

WAR DIARY

of

HEADQUARTERS
R.E.
41st DIVISION

JANUARY 1919

WAR DIARY
or
INTELLIGENCE SUMMARY. Hqrs. R.E. 6th Division

Army Form C. 2118.

JANUARY 1919

Place	Date	Hour	Summary of Events and Information	Remarks and references to Appendices
VINALMONT	1.		CRE (Lt Col. A.C. Howard M.C. R.E.) visited Field Coy R.E. at MOTTA.	
"	4.		Orders received for move to COLOGNE for relief of 1st Canadian Division on COLOGNE BRIDGEHEAD	
"	5.		CRE held conference of Field Coy Commanders	
"	6.		CRE attended Chief Engineer's conference at 4th Army HQrs	
"	7.		NAMUR Hqrs R.E. entrained with 237th Field Coy R.E. at ANDENNE.	
COLOGNE	8.		Hqrs R.E. detrained at BENSBERG and marched to COLOGNE where this office was established at 17 Robert Heuser Strasse MARIENBURG (CÖLN); billets were found by Camp Commandant, 1st Canadian Division	
"	10		228th Field Coy arrived in the COLOGNE area and took over billets at KALK	
"	11		233rd Field Coy arrived at WAHN.	
"	13.		CRE visited Field Corps	
"	15		"	

Army Form C. 2118.

WAR DIARY
or
INTELLIGENCE SUMMARY.
(Erase heading not required.)

HQrs. RE 41st Division

JANUARY 1919

Place	Date	Hour	Summary of Events and Information	Remarks and references to Appendices
COLOGNE	17		CRE visited 228th Field Coy RE at KALK	
"	18		CRE visited 233rd Field Coy RE at WAHN	
"	20		CRE visited 228th Field Coy at KALK	
"	21		CRE visited 233 Field Coy at WAHN and 237 Field Coy RE at FORSBACH	
"	23		Adjutant left for U.K. (30 days leave)	
"	25		CRE inspected 228th Field Coy RE at DEUTZ	
"	26		CRE inspected 233rd Field Coy RE at WAHN	
"	27		CRE inspected 237th Field Coy RE at FORSBACH	
"	29		CRE visited forward area and outpost line on Bk. of Cologne BRIDGEHEAD	
"	31		CRE visited 233 Field Coy RE	

Egan Capt.
Adjutant RE for Lt Col
CRE 41st Divn

CONFIDENTIAL

WAR DIARY
— OF —
HEADQUARTERS R.E.
51st DIVISION

FEBRUARY
—1919—

Army Form C. 2118.

WAR DIARY
or
INTELLIGENCE SUMMARY.
(Erase heading not required.)

HQrs RE 1st Division

FEBRUARY 1919

Place	Date	Hour	Summary of Events and Information	Remarks and references to Appendices
COLOGNE	2.		CRE visited 225th & 237th Field Coy RE. at KALK and FORSBACH	
"	3		CRE visited outpost line COLOGNE BRIDGEHEAD with a view to the commencement of defence work in connection with this line	
"	5		CRE visited forward Divisional Area; work of Slating Line of Resistance was commenced with GSO.1; the erection of wire entanglements and concrete pill boxes for machine guns (MOIR TYPE) also considered	
"	6		CRE visited 225th Field Coy RE	
"	7		" " 233rd and 237th Field Coys RE	
"	8		CRE visited outpost line in neighbourhood of ENGELSKIRCHEN	
"	10		CRE visited Field Coys RE in connection with erection of drawing chambers in Divisional Area.	

WAR DIARY
or
INTELLIGENCE SUMMARY. (Erase heading not required.)

Army Form C. 2118.

HqRs 1st Division

FEBRUARY 1919

Place	Date	Hour	Summary of Events and Information	Remarks and references to Appendices
COLOGNE	11		CRE visited forward area at MARIAHINDEN in connection with defence scheme	
"	13		CRE visited CE I Corps	
"	14		CRE visited Area Coy RE	
"	16		CRE visited outpost line and proposed line of resistance in connection with Stoney D'Esire	
"	20		and strong points	
"	22		Sites for dumps for above work were chosen at OVERATH, UNTER VILKERATH and LINDLAR	
"	23		CRE visited Field Coys RE	
"	24		CRE visited CE II Army	
"	25		CRE visited outpost line and line of resistance with GOC 1st Division and G.S.O.1	
"	27		Adjutant moved from rear	
"	28			

Jasper Capito
Adjt for Lt Colr, CRE 1st Divn

WAR DIARY or INTELLIGENCE SUMMARY

MARCH 1919   HQrs RE 4th Division

Place	Date	Hour	Summary of Events and Information	Remarks and references to Appendices
COLOGNE	1		CRE (Lt Col A.C. Howard me RE) and Adjutant (Capt. A.S. Glover RE) visited Field Coys RE and also RE dumps in forward area at OVERATH, VILKERATH and LINDLAR	
"	2		CRE visited CE II Army	
"	3		Adjutant visited 233 Field Coy RE at KALK and 228th Field Coy RE at HONRATH	
"	4		CRE visited Field Coys RE	
"	5		CE VI Corps (Brig Genl. Harvey) called	
"	6		CRE visited Field Coys RE	
"	7		CRE visited defence line in centre Brigade sector with the Divisional Commander and C.R.S.T.	
"	8		Adjutant visited 228th Field Coy RE at HONRATH also RE dumps at OVERATH, VILKERATH and LINDLAR	
"	9		CRE visited Field Coys RE	
"	10		CRE attended Divisional Commanders Conference on Training. Adjutant visited 228th Field Coy RE at HONRATH	

WAR DIARY
INTELLIGENCE SUMMARY

Headquarters RE 41st Division

MARCH 1919

Place	Date	Hour	Summary of Events and Information	Remarks and references to Appendices
COLOGNE	11		CRE visited 19th Batt Middlesex Regt at ECHSBACH.	
"	12		CRE departed to England on Demobilisation. Lt Col HA Reid DSO	
			MC assumed duties of acting CRE pending arrival of successor to Lt Col AC Howard DSO	
"	13		CRE visited defence line, 233rd Field Coys sector	
"	14		CRE & Adjutant visited defence line in 228th Field Coy sector	
"	15		CE VI Corps called. CRE & Adjutant visited DELLBRÜCK in search of materials for concrete work.	
"	17		CRE & Adjutant visited defence line in left Brigade sector with CE VI Corps	
"	18		CRE visited 233rd Field Coy HQ at HEILIGENHAUS	
"	19		CRE visited defence line in Centre Brigade sector with CE VI Corps	
"	20		CRE & Adjutant visited 2nd Army RE Park at NIPPES	
"	21		CRE visited defence line in 122nd Inf Bde sector (right) with CE VI Corps	

Army Form C. 2118.

WAR DIARY
or
INTELLIGENCE SUMMARY
(Erase heading not required.)

Hqrs. R.E. London Division

MARCH 1919

Place	Date	Hour	Summary of Events and Information	Remarks and references to Appendices
COLOGNE.	23		CRE visited 19th Batt. Middlesex Regt. (Pioneers) at ESCHBACH	
"	24		CRE visited 237th Field Coy RE at FORSBACH.	
"	26		CRE visited 228th Field Coy RE at HOVIRATH.	
"	27		CRE visited work on left Brigade sector - defence line	
"	28		Adjutant visited 2nd Army HQ Park NIPPES	
"	29		CRE & Adjutant visited CE II Corps (Brig Gen Sir Stokely DSO)	
"	31		CRE visited 19th Batt Middlesex Regt (Pios) at ESCHBACH	
			CRE (Lt Col MARRIOTT DSO in C) left for U.K. prior to demobilisation	

[signature] Capt R.E.
Adjutant for CRE London Division

CONFIDENTIAL

WAR DIARY
of
HEADQUARTERS R
LONDON DIVISION
APRIL 1919

WAR DIARY
or
INTELLIGENCE SUMMARY

Army Form C. 2118.

H. Qrs. R.E. London Division

APRIL 1919

Place	Date	Hour	Summary of Events and Information	Remarks and references to Appendices
COLOGNE	1.		Adjutant visited CE VI Corps and CE 2nd Army	
"	2		Adjutant visited work of 237 Field Coy on Rifle Range at EHRESHOVEN	
"	3		Adjutant visited Labour Commandant 2nd Army and area Commandant DEUTZ re Employment of Cologne Labour	
"	5		Adjutant visited 124th Inf. Bde. at KALK	
"	6		Adjutant visited EXERZIER PLATZ at KALK with GSO2. Also proposed Divisional Race Meeting to be held	
"	7		Adjutant visited Sharp Rifle Range at EHRESHOVEN being constructed by 237th Field Coy RE	
"	9		CRE (Lt Col Asst Lawford RE) arrived from 19th Division and assumed duties of CRE London Division. Adjutant attended Divisional Commanders Conference on Salary	
"	10		CRE & Adjutant visited 19th Middlesex (Pus), 237th Field Coy RE and 14 Qrs 123 Inf Bde.	
"	11		CRE & Adjutant visited 228 & 233 Field Coys RE & 122 Inf Bde.	

WAR DIARY
or
INTELLIGENCE SUMMARY

(Erase heading not required.)

Hqrs. CE 2nd Division

APRIL 1919

Army Form C. 2118.

Place	Date	Hour	Summary of Events and Information	Remarks and references to Appendices
COLOGNE	11		CRE & Adjutant visited CE II Corps to discuss the question of moving huts & Camps for the Division	
"	12		Adjutant visited CE Rhine Army	
"	13		CRE visited ENGELSKIRCHEN and OVERATH; work reported required on "ORR" showgrounds at this place	
"	14		CRE attended conference held by CE at Rhine Army HQrs.	
"	15		Adjutant visited CE II Corps	
"	16		CRE visited work on line of resistance in Rgr. Brigade sector BENSBERG, KALK, MÜLHEIM. CRE & Adjutant visited KALK MÜLHEIM in search of Civilian Saw-mills	
"	17		RE band visited KALK and gave two concerts for London Division	
"	19		CRE & Adjutant visited BENSBERG, arranged to take on a civilian saw mill	
"	21		CRE visited baths and disinfector at OVERATH and ENGELSKIRCHEN with ADMS.	

Army Form C. 2118.

WAR DIARY
or
INTELLIGENCE SUMMARY.
(Erase heading not required.)

Army Form C. 2118.

APRIL 1919 H.Qrs. R.E. London Division

Place	Date	Hour	Summary of Events and Information	Remarks and references to Appendices
COLOGNE	22		CRE & Adjutant visited LUSTHEIDE and installed a NCO and 10 Sappers in a saw mill there to start on RE workshop.	
"	23		CRE visited Defence Line & Cable Bryant Series and also 19th Batt. Middlesex Regt. at UNTER ESCHBACK	
"	24		CRE visited defence line on left Bryant series with OC 19th Middlesex Regt. (Pioneers)	
"	25		CRE visited HEUMAR to inspect self-closers for Camp of 4th M.G. Batalion. CRE visited OVERATH to arrange camp for 2nd Batt. Middlesex Regt.	
"	26		CRE & Adjutant visited their lines & headquarters	
"	27		CRE visited main Line of Resistance with CRE Rhine Army and CE II Corps	
"	28		CRE visited 237 Field Coy RE at FORSBACH and construction of huts for aerodrome at HEUMAR	
"	30		CRE & Adjutant visited PORZ	

T.B. Capel Lt.
A/Adjt for CRE London Div.

Army Form C. 2118.

WAR DIARY
or
INTELLIGENCE SUMMARY.
(Erase heading not required.)

Headquarters R.E. 4th Dn Division

MAY 1919

Place	Date	Hour	Summary of Events and Information	Remarks and references to Appendices
COLOGNE	1		CRE visited Site of proposed battalion Camp at VOLBERG	
"	3		CRE + Adjutant visited CE II Corps, workshops at LUSTHEIDE and M.G. Battalion Camp at HEUMAR. 2nd Lieut. D. ROSS 233 Field Co. R.E. joined Headquarters R.E. as Stores Officer.	
"	4		CRE visited 19th Batt. Middlesex Regt at UNTER ESCHBACH	
"	5		CRE attended Divisional Commanders Conference	
"	6		CRE + Adjutant visited OVERATH and HEUMAR and inspected work in progress on Battalion Camps.	
"	7		CE visited M.G. Camp at HEUMAR and R.E. workshops at LUSTHEIDE near BENSBERG	
"	8		CRE visited OVERATH. 228th Field Co. at HOFFRATH	
"	9		CRE + Lt. ROSS visited OVERATH, work in hand on Camps for 7th Batt Middlesex Regt.	
"	10		CRE, Adjutant Lt. ROSS visited EXERZIER PLATZ near KALK and Close Site for Battalion Camp.	
"	11		CRE + Adjutant visited Rifle Range at EHRESHOVEN and 5th Battn MIDDLESEX Regt. at ESCHBACH.	

Army Form C. 2118.

WAR DIARY
or
INTELLIGENCE SUMMARY.
(Erase heading not required.)

Headquarters R.E. London Division

Place	Date	Hour	Summary of Events and Information	Remarks and references to Appendices
			MAY 1919	
COLOGNE	12		CRE visited line of Residence with OC 19th Batt. Middlesex (Pnrs)	
" "	13		CRE visited line of Providence with GSO1 and OC 41st Batt. M.G.C.	
			Adjutant visited camp at HEUMAR being constructed for H.Q. Corps.	
" "	14		CRE & Adjutant visited sites for Camps at HEUMAR, OVERATH & ENGELSKIRCHEN also 2nd Bde HQrs at ALSBACH	
" "	15		CRE & Adjutant visited CE I Corps & Controller of Mines at Army HQrs. also 3rd Bde HQrs at ROSRATH	
" "	16		CRE visited sites chosen for Camps in 3rd Bde area.	
" "	17		CRE visited Officers Mess Villas ENGELSKIRCHEN and ENGELSKIRCHEN & Sisters Officers Villas OVERATH and EHRESHOVEN Cultrosin Camps and 2nd London Bde. HQrs. Adjutant visited RE workshops LUSTHEIDE and Transport lines at "The Meadows" at REFRATH	
" "	18		CRE & Adjutant visited M.G. Camp at HEUMAR.	
" "	19		CRE & Adjutant visited Camps at OVERATH and EHRESHOVEN	
" "	20		CRE visited proposed Camp at PLATZ with GSO1. also HQrs. 2nd London Bde. and Camps at OVERATH	

Army Form C. 2118.

WAR DIARY
or
INTELLIGENCE SUMMARY.
(Erase heading not required.)

Headquarters R.E. London Division

MAY 1919

Place	Date	Hour	Summary of Events and Information	Remarks and references to Appendices
COLOGNE	21		CRE visited Camps at OVERATH and EHRESHOVEN.	
"	22		CRE + A/Adjutant visited Camps at PLATZ FRANKENFORST, OVERATH, EHRESHOVEN, ENGELSKIRCHEN, VOLBERG and 3 Bdr. HQrs. at ROSRATH.	
"	23		CRE attended Div'l Commander's Conference. CRE held Conference with Coy. Commanders.	
"	24		V.CRE visited Camps in 3rd London Brigade Area.	
"	26		CRE + D.A.Q.M.G. visited Camps in Divisional Area.	
"	27		CRE visited shooting party. North Divisional Commander Adjutant.	
"	28		Visited CE VI Corps and RE Workshops LUSTHEIDE. CRE + Adjutant visited Camps at PLATZ and HEUMAR. Stores from visited LINDLAR and surveyed site for Battalion Camp.	
"	29		CRE visited Camps at OVERATH, KLEE and HONRATH.	
"	30		CRE visited Camps in Divisional with CE Rhine Army and CE VI Corps.	
"	31		CRE visited N.9. Battalion Camp at HEUMAR.	

Signed, A/Lt.Col, CRE London Div.

A/For Lt.Col, CRE London Div.

WAR DIARY
or
INTELLIGENCE SUMMARY.

(Erase heading not required.)

Army Form C. 2118.

Headquarters RE London Division

Place	Date	Hour	Summary of Events and Information	Remarks and references to Appendices
COLOGNE	2		CRE visited Camps in Overrath Area. Adjutant visited OC Tk Corps.	
"	3		CRE visited ENGELSKIRCHEN and EFFRESTOVEN Camps.	
"	4		CRE visited BENSBERG and OVERATH Camps. Adjutant visited OC Rhine Army to bring up an officer for appointment of Adjutant to London Division.	
"	5		CRE visited Camps at EFFRESTOVEN FRENGELSKIRCHEN and FRANKENFORST. Adjutant visited CE Tk Corps.	
"	6		CRE visited field Coys RE and work on Camps at LINDLAR.	
"	7		EFFRESTOVEN and ENGELSKIRCHEN. CRE visited OVERATH Collation Camp and EFFRESTOVEN. OC OC No 2 Park Tank Coy.	
"	8		CRE & Adjutant visited OC II Corps. Discussed RE Training field Coys unit "G".	
"	9		CRE visited BQ.D.Y.S. visited field Coy horse lines.	
"	10		CRE in Office. Capt A.S. Glover proceeded to VI Corps as S.O.R.E.	

Army Form C. 2118.

WAR DIARY
or
INTELLIGENCE SUMMARY.
(Erase heading not required.)

June 1919   Headquarters R.E. London N.

Place	Date	Hour	Summary of Events and Information	Remarks and references to Appendices
COLOGNE	10 (con)		Lt Y Kelsey reported to act as Adjutant	
	11		C.R.E with O.C. 228 Field Coy R.E visited camps re water Supply	
	12		C.R.E and Adjutant visited Yt Corps re stores.	
	13		C.R.E visited 237th Field Coy R.E. re FRANKENFORST & PRATZ Camps, 228th Field Coy R.E re R.E dump & water Supply OVERATH, 233 Field Coy R.E re ENGLESKIRCHEN and PARISSHOFEN Camps	
	14		C.R.E visited FRANKENFORST Camp re water supply, 23 Middlesex Regt re Barrack equipment and 233 Field Coy R.E re new chimney stix.	
	15		C.R.E and Adjutant visited R.E. Workshops LUSTHEIDE and HEUMAR Camp	
	16		C.R.E visited EHRESHOVEN and OVERATH camps. Saw G.S.O.1 with regard to operations	
	17		C.R.E visited 3 Field Coy's and discussed operations and made final arrangements. Orders from Iday received from G. C.R.E visited N.G G with regard to R.E	
	18		C.R.E attended divisional commanders conference. C.R.E visited 237th Field Coy R.E.	

Army Form C. 2118.

WAR DIARY
or
INTELLIGENCE SUMMARY.
(Erase heading not required.)

Headquarters R.E. London Division

Place	Date	Hour	Summary of Events and Information	Remarks and references to Appendices
	June			
COLOGNE	19		C.R.E. visited 1st 2nd and 3rd London Infantry Brigades and the Rine Field Coys R.E.	
	20		C.R.E. with the A.A.& Q.M.G. visited the 1st and 3rd London Infantry Brigades.	
	21		C.R.E. the A.A. and Q.M.G. visited camps in divisional area Addendum No 6 to London Division Order 29th received	
	22		C.R.E. visited site for musketry for D.A.P.M.	
	23		C.R.E. saw Divisional Commander with regard to billeting training of field Coys.	
	24		C.R.E. visited C.E.V Corps and discussed water supply etc for camps in divisional area	
	25		C.R.E. saw Divisional Commander with regard to training and work in camps in divisional area. C.R.E. & adjutant visited 237th Field Coy R.E. and with O.C. 237 " Field Coy visited all work under construction by 228 " Field Coy and 233 " Field C.R.E. C.R.E. discussed training of field Coys with Divisional Commander	
	26		and G.S.O.1 Proposed programme sent to G. C.R.E. saw A.A.Q.M.G.	

Army Form C. 2118.

WAR DIARY
or
INTELLIGENCE SUMMARY.
(Erase heading not required.)

HQ RE London Division

June 1919

Place	Date	Hour	Summary of Events and Information	Remarks and references to Appendices
COLOGNE	26 (cont)		about camps divisional area. Major Mellor of 237th Field Coy reported to take over as substitute for C.R.E. while on leave.	
	27		C.R.E. handed over work in divisional area to Major Mellor.	
	28		C.R.E. completed handing over to Major Mellor.	
	29		Lt Col A.N. LAWFORD proceeded on 28 days leave to UK. Major MELLOR acting C.R.E.	
	30		A/C.R.E visited 237 Field Coy and discussed work in hand. C.E.H. Corps visited C.R.E. in regard of work on camps for the immediate future, and training of 225 Field Coy R.E. A/C.R.E visited divisional commander to fix the new policy to be adopted owing to the signing of the peace treaty.	

Peter Nelson Lt R.E.
Act for I.C.d RE CRE London Division.

War Diary

SECRET.   COPY No. 11

C.R.Es ORDER No. G/1.

Reference 1/200000 Map, Sheet 59.
        (Copies to Field Coys. R.E. to follow).

1. It is possible that the Rhine Army may be called upon to advance in the near future; the primary object of any such advance will be the seizing of the RUHR basin with certain railways, the most important of which is the COLOGNE - OHLIGS - ELBERFELD - HAGEN - UNNA - line and other important lines are ALTENA - PLETTENBERG - KIRCHMUNDEN - KROMSBACH - SIEGEN - and SCHWERTE - ARNSBERG - MESCHEDE. The prevention of evacuation of rolling stock and personnel in front of our advance is essential for the working of these lines when they are in our hands.

2. The advance will commence on a day J to be notified later. Not more than 3 days notice may be expected.

3. The London Division will advance on a 1 Brigade front on J day. This will be the 2nd London Brigade, and the Brigade Group will consist of the following troops:-

    2nd London Infantry Brigade.
    1 Lancer Squadron.
    187 Bde. R.F.A. (less two 18 pdr. Battys).
    113th Siege Battery, R.G.A.
    233rd Field Coy. R.E.
    1 Coy. VIth Corps Cyclists.
    "B" Coy. 41st. M.G. Battalion.
    1 Section, 139th Field Ambulance.
    First Line Transport of Brigade Group.

    These troops will concentrate in the EHRESHOVEN-ENGELSKIRCHEN Area on J-2 day.
    The advance will be covered by Cyclists, and by Machine Guns mounted in Lorries. The remaining dismounted personnel will advance in busses.

Acknowledge

4. The Support Brigade Group will be 3rd London Brigade, consisting of the following :-

>3rd London Infantry Brigade.
>2 - 18 pdr. Battys, 187 Bde. R.F.A.
>159th Heavy Battery, R.G.A.
>228th Field Coy. R.E.
>"A" Coy. 41st M.G. Battalion.
>140th Field Ambulance.
>1st Line Transport, 3rd Brigade Group.
>Detachment Corps Signals.

These will concentrate in the vicinity of OVERATH on J-1 day.
On J Day they will march to GUMMERSBACH and on J + 1 day to the vicinity of HERSCHEID.

5. The Reserve Brigade Group will consist of the following

>1st London Inf. Bde.
>190th Brigade R.F.A.
>237th Field Coy. R.E.
>41st Bn M.G. Corps (less 2 Coys).
>1st Line Transport.

This Group will entrain in COLOGNE area on J + 1 day, detrain at ALTENA and march to SUNDERN - PALVE Area. The ramining troops of the Division will follow by rail on J + 2, 3 & 4 days.

6. The following orders regarding the advance have been issued :-

(a) All troops encountered will at once be disarmed, any attempt at resistance will be dealt with immediately.

(b) R.E. personnel will accompany the leading troops of each Brigade Group to search for booby traps, mines &c.

(c) A guard will be put on any train encountered to prevent it's escape into the unoccupied area.
Guards will be posted (each under an Officer) at points A, B, C, D & E on attached map and the nearest German Railway officials will be warned that a rail has been removed at each of these points to prevent trains escaping.
These guards will remain until the arrival of the British Railway personnel to take over control of railways (see attached map).

(d) Every formation is resposible for it's own protection against surprise.
All transport personnel will be armed and Officers will always carry revolvers.

(e) All transport will be provided with an escort.

(7/-).

7. Motor Cyclist Despatch riders will maintain touch with Brigade Groups moving by road and with VI Corps. Units will make full use of cyclist orderlies and detail suitable men as mounted orderlies. Units, on arrival at their destination each day, should make a point of informing all ranks on parade of the position of the Unit or formation Headquarters; this will greatly assist Despatch Riders making enquiries.

8. Field Coys. R.E. will operate under the orders of G.O.C. Infantry Brigade to which they are attached until a stationary position is taken up when they will come under orders of C.R.E. Field Coy. Commanders will endeavour to send back any useful information to this office by whatever means are available, also their location daily.
Advanced Divisional Headquarters will open at 8.00 hours on J day at ALSBACH SCHLOSS near ENGELSKIRCHEN and at LUDENSCHEID at 12.00 hours on J+1 day.
On receipt of orders from this office, O.C. 237th Field Coy. R.E. will despatch 10 Sappers on cycles for attachment to 233rd Field Coy. R.E.
On J-3 day the R.E. Workshops will be disbanded and tools in stock will be sent to OVERATH R.E. Dump.
On J-3 day personnel of 233rd Field Coy. R.E. at OVERATH Dump will rejoin their Coy; on J-2 the personnel of 228th Field Coy. R.E. will rejoin their Unit from OVERATH Dump.

9. SUPPLIES. One Coy. Divisional Train will concentrate with each Brigade Group.

   (a) 2nd Brigade Group. Troops will embus with unexpired portion of the days rations on the man, and preserved rations for J+1 day will be taken on the busses under Unit arrangements. Rations for a further 2 days will be sent by M.T. in charge of Brigade Supply officer with the Brigade Group busses.

   (b) 3rd Brigade Group. Unexpired portion of the days ration on the man, and rations for J+1 day on first line transport or on the man. Supply wagons will travel loaded with rations for J+2 day. Rendezvous for rations for consumption on J+3 day will be road junction H.4.1.7, South of LENGELSCHEID, near Station at 16.00 hours.

SUPPLIES continued.

(c). Rations will be drawn from refilling point on J day for consumption J ∓ 2 day with First Line Transport. Units will entrain with unexpired portion of days rations plus rations for J ∓ 2 day.
Rations for consumption J ∓ 3 day will be delivered by lorry on J ∓ 1 day to BALVE when a Dump will be formed. Refilling will be by First Line Transport on J ∓ 2 day under Brigade arrangements.

10. **AMMUNITION.**

This will be issued under Brigade arrangements.

11. **SURPLUS KITS.**

Troops proceeding by bus will only take with them those stores they can carry on arrival at destination as no other transport will be available in time to move kits from debussing points.
All units will move with baggage and equipment as laid down in Mob. Store Table.
All equipment, clothing and Ordnance stores surplus to above will be returned through D.A.D.O.S. to Corps Ordnance Intermediate Collecting Stations. Duplicate lists will be furnished by Units.
All stores, etc, surplus to above will be concentrated in Central Dumps in Brigade Areas and will be left in charge of a small guard; Field Coys. should arrange with Brigades for their surplus kits to be placed in these Dumps. Strength of guards and location of Dumps will be reported at once to D.H.Q., in order that rations may be arranged. Brigades will leave rations for these guards on J and J ∓ 1 days; they will also be in possession of iron rations. 5 Lorries will report to each Brigade Headquarters on J - 3 day by 16.00 hours and be at the disposal of Brigades for concentrating stores. They must not return to park later than 18.00 hours J - 1 day.
Surplus kit to be placed in these Dumps.

12. **BLANKETS AND PACKS.**

No blankets will be taken. Packs will be carried on the men except by 3rd Brigade Group for whom Lorries will be provided.

13. D.A.D.O.S. will move to LUDENSCHEID on J ∓ 2 day.

14. Mobile Vetinary Section will move with 3rd Bde. Group.

15. Guards will be left on all tent damps. Isolated tents will be placed in Dumps - see para 11.

16. Extract from entraining table for J ∓ 1 day (1st Bde. Group)

Train No.	Entrng. Str.	Times Load.	Dep.	Unit.
3.	KALK.	07.30.	08.00	237th Fld. Coy. R.E. H.Q. plus Coy. M.G. Bn.
9.	MULHEIM.	15.00	18.00	Transport H.Qrs. plus 1 Coy. M.G. Bn. 237th Field Coy. R.E.

Detraining station will be ALTENA.

1-6- 1919.

Lieut-Colonel R.E.,
C.R.E. London Div.

S E C R E T. APPENDIX "A" (Issued with C.R.E. London Division Order No. G.1 dated 31/5/19).

Serial No.	Date.	Unit.	From	To	Remarks.
1.	J - 2 day.	2nd Ldn. Inf. Bde. Group.	Concentrates in Area EHRESHOVEN - ENGELSKIRCHEN - LINDLAR.		
2.	J - 1 day.	3rd Ldn. Bde. Group.	Concentrates in Area round OVERATH.		
3.	J day.	2nd Ldn. Bde. Group.	ENGELSKIRCHEN Area	NEUERUCKE - ATTENDORN - OLPE Area.	Move by bus via NEUSTADT.
4.	J day.	3rd Ldn. Bde. Group.	OVERATH Area.	GUMMERSBACH - NEUSTADT Area.	Move by March route.
5.	J + 1 day.	2nd Ldn. Bde. Group.	NEUERUCKE - ATTENDORN OLPE Area.	MESCHEDE - ARNSBERG - HUSTEN Area.	Move by bus via SUNDERN.
6.	J + 1 day.	3rd Ldn. Bde. Group.	GUMMERSBACH - NEUSTADT Area.	HERSCHEID - MEINERTZHAGEN Area.	Move by March route.
7.	J + 1 day.	1st Ldn. Bde. Group.	Reserve Bde. Area.	ALTENA Area.	Move by Train. Details will be issued later.
8.	J + 2 day.	3rd Ldn. Bde. Group.	HERSCHEID - MEINERTZHAGEN Area.	PLETTENBERG - NEUENRADE Area.	NEUENRADE - LANGENHOLTHAUSSEN road will be kept clear of traffic for move of 1st Ldn. Bde. Group.
9.	J + 2 day.	1st Ldn. Bde. Group.	ALTENA Area	ENDORF - HAGEN - BALVE - HACHEN - SUNDERN Area.	Move by march route on detraining at ALTENA. via NEUENRADE and LANGENHOLTHAUSSEN

DISTRIBUTION :-

1. 228th Field Coy. R.E.
2. 233rd Field Coy. R.E.
3. 237th Field Coy. R.E.
4. London Division "G".
5. London Division "Q".
6. 1st London Infantry Brigade.
7. 2nd London Infantry Brigade.
8. 3rd London Infantry Brigade.
9. 19th Bn. Middlesex Regt. (P).
10. C.E. VIth Corps.
11. War Diary.
12. File.

Army Form C. 2118.

WAR DIARY
or
INTELLIGENCE SUMMARY.
(Erase heading not required.)

Instructions regarding War Diaries and Intelligence Summaries are contained in F. S. Regs., Part II. and the Staff Manual respectively. Title pages will be prepared in manuscript.

HQ. RE London Division

JULY 1919

Place	Date	Hour	Summary of Events and Information	Remarks and references to Appendices
COLOGNE	1		a/CRE and Adjutant visited 228 Field Coy RE at MULHEIM also B Coy & Middlesex Regt who assisted 228 Field Coy (RE) in work in camps (to be completed)	
	2		o/CRE visited A.D. and I.W.T. with regard to work in hand and transfer of unit	
	3		o/CRE visited FRANKFORSST Camp, QUINCEY, c/ BENSBERG, 140 Field Coys at YNGST and 237 Field Coy RE at FORSBACH	
	4		o/CRE visited HEUMAR Camp with O.C. 59" Sanitary Section, "CRE visited 228 Field Coy, B Coy 19 Middlesex Regt at HONRATH	
	5		CRE in Office, Adjutant visited RE Workshop LUSTHEIDE	
	6		CRE visited WESTHOFEN Camp, pw OAS and objected all to section work	
	7		o/CRE visited 237 Field Coy RE	
	8		o/CRE visited O.H.G. telegraph network in divisional area	
	9		o/CRE visited 331 Field Coy RE & Bureau depot MULHEIM	
	9		o/CRE in Office	
	10		o/CRE in Office	
	11		o/CRE visited 354 E.M Coy at KLETTENBERG in lighting of Camps and 228 Field Coy RE at MULHEIM	

Army Form C. 2118.

WAR DIARY
or
INTELLIGENCE SUMMARY.
(Erase heading not required.)

HQ RE LONDON DIVISION

July 1919

Place	Date	Hour	Summary of Events and Information	Remarks and references to Appendices
COLOGNE	12	12	9/CRE in Office. 2/Lt DAVIDSON of 354 F.M Coy called to discuss lighting in Camps in divisional area. Adjutant & Store Officer visited 233 Field Coy RE + B Coy 19 Middlesex Regt at HONRATH.	
	13		9/CRE in Office. Adjutant visited 225 Field Coy RE	
	14		9/CRE visited A?TO MG + GSO.I re infantry transfers etc	
	15		a/CRE with an Officer from H.Q. 354 F.M Coy visited HEUMAR (RATH) Camp + FRANKENFORST Camp re lighting	
	16		9/CRE in Office. Adjutant visited German contractor who supplied huts to EHRESHOVEN Camp	
	17		9/CRE visited GSO.I + saw O.C. 223 Field Coy relieved situation of "B" Coy 19th Middlesex Regiment who had a detachment at MUHLHEIM Railway Detachment ordered to return	
	18		CRE in Office. Adjutant visited RE workshops LUSTHEIDE, FRANKENFORST + RATH (HEUMAR) Camp.	
	19		Bearers Holiday	
	20		9/CRE visited 237 Field Coy at forebach then RATH Camp.	

Army Form C. 2118.

WAR DIARY
or
INTELLIGENCE SUMMARY.
(Erase heading not required.)

Instructions regarding War Diaries and Intelligence Summaries are contained in F. S. Regs., Part II. and the Staff Manual respectively. Title pages will be prepared in manuscript.

HQRE LONDON DIVISION

Place	Date	Hour	Summary of Events and Information	Remarks and references to Appendices
COLOGNE	21		2/CRE visited 228 Field Coy RE for Divisional Commanders inspection. O'ERATH	
	22		Dumps 223 Field Coy RE were visited. 2/CRE visited GRO & engineer about future policy in regard to hutting. 2/CRE	
	23		visited 237 Field Coy RE. 2/CRE with Stores officer visited all forward camps in divisional area to slip all works that were not approaching completion. Coys orders is cancel work received.	
	24		2/CRE with stores officer revisited remaining camps in divisional area. Adjutant visited MT Coy RASC and attended Lecture on P.M. Bomb.	
	25		2/CRE in office. Adjutant visited RE Workshops.	
	26		2/CRE in office. Adjutant attended G.C.M. enquiries. 2/CRE visited 258 Field Coy RE.	
	27		2/CRE in office. Adjutant visited 238 Field Coy RE of Mulheim.	
	28		2/CRE attended conference at MULHEIM FORST on RADOS RASC supplies.	
	29		Adjutant visited RE workshops. 2/CRE in office. Lt Col AN LAWFORD returned from leave RUK.	
	30		CRE took over from Major MELLOR. Adjutant visited RE workshops.	
	31		CRE (A975) took over from Major MELLOR.	

Tietur Wampert for Lt Col RE CRE London Division.

Army Form C. 2118.

WAR DIARY
or
INTELLIGENCE SUMMARY.
(Erase heading not required.)

HQ RE LONDON DIVISION

AUGUST 1919

Place	Date	Hour	Summary of Events and Information	Remarks and references to Appendices
COLOGNE	1		CRE completed taking over from Major Mellor	
	2		CRE in office	
	3		Adjutant visited EHRESHOVEN & OVERATH musketry camps. Major Mellor left for UK	
	4		Holiday. CRE visited 237 Field Coy	
	5		CRE visited 233 Field Coy at MULHEIM, 228 Field Coy at HONRATH, & Transport Lines of 233 Field Coy at AVIKERATH. Also FRANKENFORST EHRESHOVEN and OVERATH Camps	
	6		CRE in office and visited AA QMG, + GO C work regard to OVERATH RE Dump	
	7		CRE visited 228 Field Coy RE w/r regard their inspection, 233 Field Coy Transport at UNTER-YULGERATH, EHRESHOVEN Battn Camp and FRANKENFORST	
	8		CRE visited ~~Major~~ D190 Bde D A at POLL with staff. Capt D.A. Adjutant Capt V. Kersey proceeded on leave tour. Lt D Ross Acting Adjutant (CC 233 Field Coy north of Training)	
	9		CRE inspected 228th Field Coy RE and visited RATH, ROSRATH HQ VILBERG HOFFNUNGSTHAL and OVERATH Camps accompanied by Adjutant	
	10		CRE visited LOW AV A+G; CRE in office	

Army Form C. 2118.

WAR DIARY
or
INTELLIGENCE SUMMARY.
(Erase heading not required.)

AUGUST 1919.   H.Q. R.E. LONDON DIVIS[ION]

Place	Date	Hour	Summary of Events and Information	Remarks and references to Appendices
Cologne	11		CRE with 232nd Field Coy RE Inspected at Mulheim, also 233rd Field Coy RE riding out at Vilkerath - 228th & 237th (less at Honrath and Forsbach)	
	12		CRE visited Frankenforst and Rath Camps - RE Workshops	
	13		Inspection by G.O.C. of 228th Field Coy RE at Honrath. CRE present.	
	14		CRE visited 237th Field Coy RE Forsbach & inspected transport.	
			CRE visited Wahn Barracks re making accommodation for Concentration of 3rd Army Corps.	
	15		C.R.E. in office	
	16		In office	
	17		In office	
	18		Visited Limmelau re bath-house. Frankenforst Camp - Bensberg Barracks & Overath Bn Camp.	
	19		In office	
	20		CRE visited AT Workshop. Frankenforst Camp. 16th Queens. 24th Bn Royal Fusiliers - Ermeshoven Camp - Lindlar Baths -	
	21		In office	

Army Form C. 2118.

WAR DIARY
or
INTELLIGENCE SUMMARY.
(Erase heading not required.)

Instructions regarding War Diaries and Intelligence Summaries are contained in F. S. Regs., Part II. and the Staff Manual respectively. Title pages will be prepared in manuscript.

Place	Date	Hour	Summary of Events and Information	Remarks and references to Appendices
Cologne	22		CRE visited II Corps CE also R.A.T.H Camp re baths + RE Workshops	
Cologne	23		LOSTHEIDE. O/say visited RE Workshops	
			CRE visited 19th B. Marlox IMMEKEPPEL and LINDLAR-FRITH	
	24		Recon parties to Mayrshot	
	25		CRE visited London Bus A - CRE in Office	
			CRE in office	
	26		CRE visited WAHN to fix billets for divisional RE also R.A.T.H Camps. Adjutant took over from o/say on return from leave.	
	27		CRE visited No 1 Camp WAHN. CRE visited VOLBERG Camp, 3rd Ech HQ, No 12th Coys & London Div TRAIN and OVERATH Dump	
	28		CRE visited camps in Divisional area to obtain working of accommodation etc	
	29		HQ RE moved from COLOGNE to No 1 Prisoners of War Camp WAHN	
WAHN	30		CRE attended Divisional Commanders conference	
	31		CRE held conference of Coy commanders, Major McGill. O.C.	

WAR DIARY
or
INTELLIGENCE SUMMARY.

(Erase heading not required.)

Army Form C. 2118.

Place	Date	Hour	Summary of Events and Information	Remarks and references to Appendices
WAHN	31		228 Field Coy RE — Major S. PLATTEN OC 233 Field Coy and Major JONES OC 237 Field Coy and he adjulated attended the policy for the removal of the two field Coys concentrated at WAHN and 237 Field Coy at MULHEIM was discussed. Colonel AN HANFORD received orders to proceed to England forthwith to report to AG7 War Office	

Peter K Kley
Capt RE
for CRE Lincoln Division.

Army Form C. 2118.

WAR DIARY
or
INTELLIGENCE SUMMARY.
(Erase heading not required.)

HQ RE London Division

Place	Date	Hour	Summary of Events and Information	Remarks and references to Appendices
WAHN			Sept 1919	
	1		CRE handed over to Major S PLOTTER and proceeded to U.K. to report to A.G.7. War Office.	
	2		a/CRE visited OVERATH, RE Workshops HUSTHEIDE, HEUMAR, also London Division Q & G.S.O.3.	
	3		a/CRE in office. G.O.C. London Division inspected N°1 Prisoners of War Camp	
	4		a/CRE attended a meeting Morden Du HORSE SHOW Committee and inspected the HORSE SHOW GROUND OVERATH	
	5		a/CRE visited OVERATH and HUSTHEIDE, 237 Field Coy RE & London Division Q.	
	6		a/CRE inspected N°1 Prisoners of War Camp WAHN	
	7		a/CRE in office	
	8		a/CRE and adjutant visited 2nd London Inf/Bde SIEGBURG Forest Camp LOHMAR, OVERATH Dump, M.G. Camp Rale 3rd London Inf Bde ROSRATH & 52 MY.S. KALK.	
	9		a/CRE in office.	
	10		a/CRE visited D.A.Q.O.S., N°4 A.S.C. Coy and 237 Field Coy MULHEIM	

Army Form C. 2118.

WAR DIARY
or
INTELLIGENCE SUMMARY.
(Erase heading not required.)

Sept 1919   HQ RE London DIVISION

Place	Date	Hour	Summary of Events and Information	Remarks and references to Appendices
WAHN	11		a/CRE in office. Lt-Col Prior acting CE K Corps called	
	12		a/CRE attended London Div Horse Show committee meeting visited Q, A, & G. re Training and clearing RE Dumps.	
	13		a/CRE inspected N°1 Prisoners of war Camp WAHN.	
	14		a/CRE visited 237 Field Coy. Lt-Col Prior acting CE K Corps called at WAHN to discuss future policy.	
	15		a/CRE in office	
	16		London Divisional Horse Show.	
	17		a/CRE in office.	
	18		a/CRE in office.	
	19		a/CRE and adjutant visited CE K Corps, London Division "A", D.A.D.O.S, + 237 Field Coy. also OVERATH Dump + LOHMAR Camp.	
	20		a/CRE +adjutant visited 2nd London Fd Bde H.Q. + Civil Dutiu SIEGBURG.	
	21		a/CRE in office	
	22		a/CRE visited HNO DYNAMITE Factory + LOHMAR Camp to pass work done by German Contractors	

Army Form C. 2118.

WAR DIARY
or
INTELLIGENCE SUMMARY.
(Erase heading not required.)

Instructions regarding War Diaries and Intelligence Summaries are contained in F. S. Regs., Part II. and the Staff Manual respectively. Title pages will be prepared in manuscript.

SEPT. 1919.   HQ. RE London Division

Place	Date	Hour	Summary of Events and Information	Remarks and references to Appendices
WAHN	23		a/CRE visited RATH Camp, VOLBERG + HOFFNUNGSTAL. EHRESHOVEN + 37 Field Coy MÜLHEIM.	
	24		a/CRE visited BENSBERG Barrack & London Division. QtG.	
	25		a/CRE visited MARIENBURG Barracks in regard to their accommodation.	
	26,27,28		a/CRE in Office.	
	29		a/CRE visited SIEGBURG, to inspect billet 8/2/4 Queen's Regt.	
	30		a/CRE to adjutant visited Requisition Officer SIEGBURG.	

Peter Kilroy
Captain
f. CRE London Division.

Army Form C. 2118.

333/

WAR DIARY
or
INTELLIGENCE SUMMARY.

(Erase heading not required.)

LONDON DIVISION

October

Place	Date	Hour	Summary of Events and Information	Remarks and references to Appendices
MULHEIM	1		CRE in office. Lt Col Prior called	
	2		237 Field Coy moved GRAFFEN from MULHEIM	
	3		CRE visited G.S.O.1 discusses reductions of the field Coy	
	4		Divisional RE moved from No 1 Prisoners of War Camp to Permanent Artillery Barracks WATTIN. HQ to No 2 Staff Officers Barracks. Lt Col Prior called	
	5		CRE in office	
	6		CRE visits A Q.M.G with regard Grassby overstocks transport area stored outfuries	
	7		CRE & adjutant visited OVERATH, ENGELSKIRCHEN, BENSBERG	
	8		CRE in office. Lt Col Prior called	
	9		CRE attended Divisional Commanders Conference on the situation of the Rhine Army	
	10		CRE in office	
	11		CRE visited SIEGBURG	
	12		CRE in office	

WAR DIARY
or
INTELLIGENCE SUMMARY.

Army Form C. 2118.

HQ RE London District

Oct 1919

Place	Date	Hour	Summary of Events and Information	Remarks and references to Appendices
WAHN.	13		CRE visited E in C with regard to reduction of Field Coys	
	14		CRE visited FORSBERG + ROSRATH also FRANKENFORST Camp	
	15		CRE in office. OVERATH RE Dump handed over to German Coal authorities	
	16		CRE visited Division	
	17		CRE in office. Capt Innes left 237 Field Coy to join 206 = Field Coy	
	20		CRE installation C + Command Paymaster	
	19		CRE in office	
	18		CRE in office 9 AM. Lt Col Prior called re reorganisation of Rhine Army	
	21		CRE circulated new Staff Capt in 1, 2 + 3 Sub areas Island Com receipt note for new requisitions. E in C to 228 Field Coy to be Kenzen disposed of. LOHMAR FOREST Camp to be taken over done by German Contractor. CRE held a conference	
	22		OC 228, 233, 237 Field Coys to and adjusted establ[ishment] Orders issued for Field Coys to commence 233+237 Field Coys to let last 228 Field Coy letter reorganisg. (Authority Rhine Army NE A6/4/214 (0))	Appendix 1

Army Form C. 2118.

WAR DIARY
or
INTELLIGENCE SUMMARY. HQ RE Lahore Division

(Erase heading not required.)

Instructions regarding War Diaries and Intelligence Summaries are contained in F.S. Regs., Part II. and the Staff Manual respectively. Title pages will be prepared in manuscript.

Month: Oct 1919

Place	Date	Hour	Summary of Events and Information	Remarks and references to Appendices
WAHN	23		233rd Field Coys Equipment handed in ¾CRE workshops	
	24		¾CRE in office	
	25		¾CRE in office. Divisional RE workshops cleared up & handed to 228 Field Coy	
	26		Major S. Platten ¾CRE took over temporarily 225 Field Coy from Major McGill.	
	27		Personnel sent from 228, 233rd & 291st Field Coys to 231st Field Coy/114SAT Coy	
	28		Orders for Cross Posting. Officers received. Major S. Platten appointed O.C. 228 Field Coy	
	29		Major S. Platten visited divisional to see by whom 228 Field Coy would be administered. Detachment of 233 & 291 Field Coys completed.	
	30		Major S. Platten gazetted a/Lt. Col. Colonel, CRE Lahore Division (a/Lt Col H) Lt-Col Prior called & gave orders for Capt Y. Kersey to proceed to his HQ at E. Coys.	
	31		HQ CE Lahore Division destroyed Board of Officers ordered on appendix 2. attached set to order the disposal of a few documents & correspondence	

S. Platten Lt Col
CRE Lahore Div.

www.ingramcontent.com/pod-product-compliance
Lightning Source LLC
Chambersburg PA
CBHW081549160426
43191CB00011B/1877